Country
CROSS STITCH

Country
CROSS STITCH

GAIL BUSSI

SUSIE JOHNS

CHRISTINA MARSH

MEREHURST

The projects in this book were all stitched with DMC stranded cotton
embroidery threads with the exception of projects on the following
pages, which were stitched with Anchor stranded cotton embroidery threads:
pp 12-15, 28-31, 68-75, 80-87, 92-99, 104-107 and 112-115.
The keys given with each chart also list combinations for those who wish to use
alternative brand threads, DMC, Anchor and Madeira, to those used for the project.

Published in 1995 by Merehurst Limited
Ferry House, 51-57 Lacy Road, Putney, London SW15 1PR
© Copyright 1995 Merehurst Limited
ISBN 1 85391 555 6

A catalogue record for this book is available from the British Library.

Edited by Diana Lodge and Heather Dewhurst
Designed by Maggie Aldred
Photography by Marie Louise Avery
Illustrations by John Hutchinson
Reformatted by Samantha Gray and Shiela Volpe
Typesetting by Dacorum Type & Print, Hemel Hempstead
Colour separation by Fotographics Limited, UK – Hong Kong
Printed in Singapore by Toppan Printing Co.

*Merehurst is the leading publisher of craft books and has an excellent range
of titles to suit all levels. Please send to the address above for our
free catalogue, stating the title of this book.*

CONTENTS

$\mathscr{I}$NTRODUCTION

Cottages, flowers, the effect of the changing seasons on the landscape and the delightful creatures of the wild are all enduring sources of inspiration for the embroiderer. Somehow embroidery threads, with their luscious colours, and fine stitchery are ideal for capturing the many delicate hues and picturesque details found in the countryside.

The projects in this book celebrate the glorious variety of the countryside – the traditions of village life, seasonal landscapes, the beauty of cottage garden flowers, wild flowers and woodland plants and trees, animal wildlife and pretty cottages.

As well as framing the finished project to make a decorative picture, there are lots of ideas for making useful items for the home such as a tray, tea cosy, tablecloth or bath set. For someone special, you may like to make a cross stitch greeting card – sure to be kept and framed!

Even if you have never done cross stitch before, this book will enable you to master all the techniques you need to know. Just follow the instructions in the Basic Skills section to get started and, in no time, you will have gained confidence and realised the joy of the craft.

The simplicity of cross stitch is belied by the intricate and exquisite effects that can be achieved – just like painting with a needle and thread. Even beginners will be surprised and delighted with the results they achieve, although it's sensible to choose a reasonably simple project for your first attempt. For experienced cross stitchers, there will be a wealth of temptation in this beautiful and instructive book so, whatever your level of skill, get stitching!

BASIC SKILLS

BEFORE YOU BEGIN

PREPARING THE FABRIC

Even with an average amount of handling, many evenweave fabrics tend to fray at the edges, so it is a good idea to overcast the raw edges, using ordinary sewing thread, before you begin.

FABRIC

Some projects in this book use Aida fabric, which is ideal both for beginners and more advanced stitchers as it has a surface of clearly designated squares. All Aida fabric has a count, which refers to the number of squares (each stitch covers one square) to one inch (2.5cm); the higher the count, the smaller the finished stitching. The projects in this book use 11-, 14- or 18-count Aida, popular and readily available sizes, in a wide variety of colours. Linen has been used for several projects in this book; although less simple to stitch on than Aida fabric (because you need to count over a specified number of threads) it does give a very attractive, traditional finish. The most commonly available linen has 28 threads to 2.5cm (1in), which when worked over two threads gives a stitch count of 14 to 2.5cm (1in).

THE INSTRUCTIONS

Each project begins with a full list of the materials that you will require. The measurements given for the embroidery fabric include a minimum of 5cm (2in) all around to allow for stretching it in a frame and preparing the edges to prevent them from fraying.

Colour keys for stranded embroidery cottons – DMC, Anchor or Madeira – are given with each chart. It is assumed that you will need to buy one skein of each colour mentioned in a particular key, even though you may use less, but where two or more skeins are needed, this information is included in the main list of requirements.

To work from the charts, particularly those where several symbols are used in close proximity, some readers may find it helpful to have the chart enlarged so that the squares and symbols can be seen more easily. Many photocopying services will do this for a minimum charge.

Before you begin to embroider, always mark the centre of the design with two lines of basting stitches, one vertical and one horizontal, running from edge to edge of the fabric, as indicated by the arrows on the charts.

As you stitch, use the centre lines given on the chart and the basting threads on your fabric as reference points for counting the squares and threads to position your design accurately.

WORKING IN A HOOP

A hoop is the most popular frame for use with small areas of embroidery. It consists of two rings, one fitted inside the other; the outer ring usually has an adjustable screw attachment so that it can be tightened to hold the stretched fabric in place. Hoops are available in several sizes, ranging from 10cm (4in) in diameter to quilting hoops with a diameter of 38cm (15in). Hoops with table stands or floor stands attached are also available.

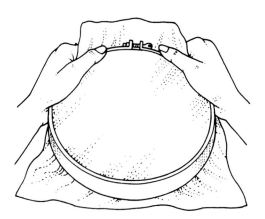

1 To stretch your fabric in a hoop, place the area to be embroidered over the inner ring and press the outer ring over it, with the tension screw released. Tissue paper can be placed between the outer ring and the embroidery, so that the hoop does not mark the fabric. Lay the tissue paper over the fabric when you set it in the hoop, then tear away the central embroidery area.

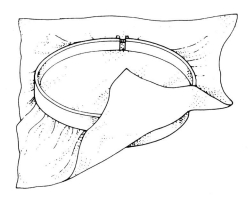

2 Smooth the fabric and, if necessary, straighten the grain before tightening the screw. The fabric should be evenly stretched.

WORKING IN A RECTANGULAR FRAME

Rectangular frames are more suitable for larger pieces of embroidery. They consist of two rollers, with tapes attached, and two flat side pieces, which slot into the rollers and are held in place by pegs or screw attachments. Available in different sizes, either alone or with adjustable table or floor stands, frames are measured by the length of the roller tape, and range in size from 30cm (12in) to 68cm (27in).

As alternatives to a slate frame, canvas stretchers and the backs of old picture frames can be used. Provided there is sufficient extra fabric around the finished size of the embroidery, the edges can be turned under and simply attached with drawing pins (thumb tacks) or staples.

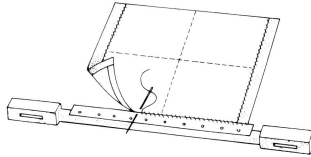

1 To stretch your fabric in a rectangular frame, cut out the fabric, allowing at least an extra 5cm (2in) all around the finished size of the embroidery. Baste a single 12mm (½in) turning on the top and bottom edges and oversew strong tape, 2.5cm (1in) wide, to the other two sides. Mark the centre line both ways with basting stitches. Working from the centre outward and using strong thread, oversew the top and bottom edges to the roller tapes. Fit the side pieces into the slots, and roll any extra fabric on one roller until the fabric is taut.

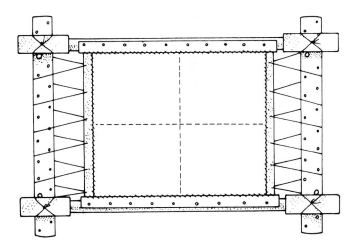

2 Insert the pegs or adjust the screw attachments to secure the frame. Thread a large-eyed needle (chenille needle) with strong thread or fine string and lace both edges, securing the ends around the intersections of the frame. Lace the webbing at 2.5cm (1in) intervals, stretching the fabric evenly.

EXTENDING EMBROIDERY FABRIC

It is easy to extend a piece of embroidery fabric, such as a bookmark, to stretch it in a hoop.

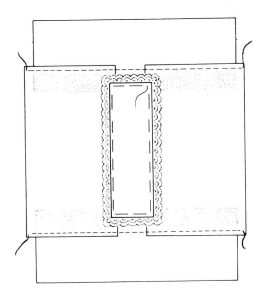

● Fabric oddments of a similar weight can be used. Simply cut four pieces to size (in other words, to the measurement that will fit both the embroidery fabric and your hoop) and baste them to each side of the embroidery fabric before stretching it in the hoop in the usual way.

TO BIND AN EDGE

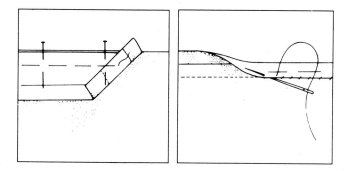

Open out the turning on one edge of the bias binding and pin in position on the right side of the fabric, matching the fold to the seamline. Fold over the cut end of the binding. Finish by overlapping the starting point by about 12mm ($\frac{1}{2}$in). Baste and machine stitch along the seam. Fold the binding over the raw edge to the wrong side, baste and, using matching sewing thread, hem neatly to finish.

MOUNTING EMBROIDERY

The cardboard should be cut to the size of the finished embroidery, with an extra 6mm ($\frac{1}{4}$in) added all round to allow for the recess in the frame.

LIGHTWEIGHT FABRICS

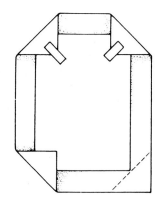 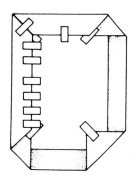

1 Place embroidery face down, with the cardboard centred on top, and basting and pencil lines matching. Begin by folding over the fabric at each corner and securing it with masking tape.

2 Working first on one side and then the other, fold over the fabric on all sides and secure it firmly with pieces of masking tape, placed about 2.5cm (1in) apart. Also neaten the mitred corners with masking tape, pulling the fabric tightly to give a firm, smooth finish.

HEAVIER FABRICS

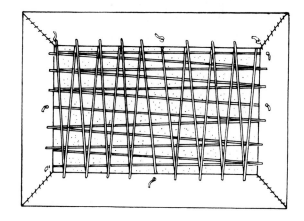

● Lay the embroidery face down, with the cardboard centred on top; fold over the edges of the fabric on opposite sides, making mitred folds at the corners, and lace across, using strong thread. Repeat on the other two sides. Finally, pull up the fabric firmly over the cardboard. Overstitch the mitred corners.

CROSS STITCH

For all cross stitch embroidery, the following two methods of working are used. In each case, neat rows of vertical stitches are produced on the back of the fabric.

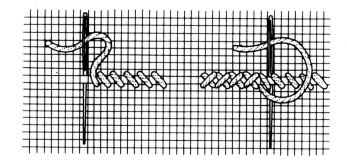

● When stitching large areas, work in horizontal rows. Working from right to left, complete the first row of evenly spaced diagonal stitches over the number of threads specified in the project instructions. Then, working from left to right, repeat the process. Continue in this way, making sure each stitch crosses in the same direction.

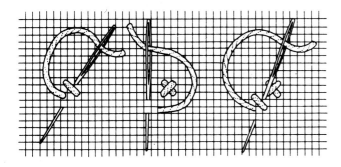

● When stitching diagonal lines, work downwards, completing each stitch before moving to the next. When starting a project always begin to embroider at the centre of the design and work outwards to ensure that the design will be placed centrally on the fabric.

THREE-QUARTER CROSS STITCHES

Some fractional stitches are used on certain projects in this book; although they strike fear into the hearts of less experienced stitchers they are not difficult to master, and give a more natural line in certain instances. Should you find it difficult to pierce the centre of the Aida block, simply use a sharp needle to make a small hole in the centre first.

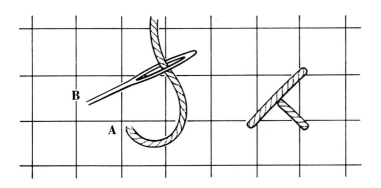

To work a three-quarter cross, bring the needle up at point A and down through the centre of the square at B. Later, the diagonal back stitch finishes the stitch. A chart square with two different symbols separated by a diagonal line requires two 'three-quarter' stitches. Backstitch will later finish the square.

A clear distinction needs to be made between three-quarter stitches and half cross stitches, which have been used in a number of projects in this book.

A three-quarter stitch occupies half of a square diagonally. A half cross stitch is like a normal cross stitch, but only the top stitch is worked, to give a more delicate effect. Stitches worked in this way are indicated quite clearly on the colour keys with their own symbols

FRENCH KNOTS

This stitch is shown on some of the diagrams by a small dot. Where there are several french knots, the dots have been omitted to avoid confusion. Where this occurs you should refer to the instructions of the project and the colour photograph.

To work a french knot, bring your needle and cotton out slightly to the right of where you want your french knot to be. Wind the thread once or twice around the needle, depending on how big you want your knot to be, and insert the needle to the left of the point where you brought it out.

Be careful not to pull too hard or the knot will disappear through the fabric. The instructions state the number of strands of cotton to be used for the french knots.

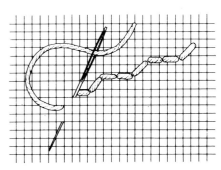

BACKSTITCH

Backstitch is used in the projects to give emphasis to a particular foldline, an outline or a shadow. The stitches are worked over the same number of threads as the cross stitch, forming continuous straight or diagonal lines.

● Make the first stitch from left to right; pass the needle behind the fabric and bring it out one stitch length ahead to the left. Repeat and continue in this way along the line.

$\mathcal{V}$ILLAGE LIFE

Capture the picturesque landmarks and charming traditions of village life in cross stitch with the projects in this section. There are five pictures – a church, the characteristic village inn, and three cottages – put them together and you have the essence of a typical small hamlet.

COUNTRY VILLAGE

YOU WILL NEED

For either the *Church* or the *Inn*, each set in a frame with a centre measuring
11.5cm × 7.5cm (4½in × 3in):

*25cm × 17.5cm (10in × 7in) of blue,
14-count Aida fabric
Stranded embroidery cotton in the colours given
in the appropriate panel
No26 tapestry needle
Picture frame, with a cut-out as specified above
Firm card, to fit the frame
Lightweight synthetic batting, the same size
as the card
Masking tape for mounting
Glue stick*

For each house/cottage picture, each set in a frame
with a centre measuring 7.5cm (3in) square:

*17.5cm (7in) square of blue, 14-count Aida fabric
Picture frame with a cut-out as specified above.
Stranded embroidery cotton, tapestry needles, firm
card, synthetic batting, masking tape and glue, as for
Church and Inn.*

*NOTE: if you are making all five pictures at the same
time, you will find that 46cm × 38cm (18in × 15in)
of Aida fabric will be sufficient. One skein of stranded
cotton in each of the colours listed on the charts will
be sufficient to complete all five designs; if you wish
to embroider a single design, buy only the colours
indicated on the relevant chart.*

•

THE EMBROIDERY

Prepare the edges of the fabric as dexcribed on page
8. If you are making all five designs, baste along the
lines separating the five pictures, ensuring that you
leave a margin of fabric around each picture area
for mounting (see below), but do not cut the fabric.
Baste horizontal and vertical centre lines across
each section to mark the centre of each picture area.
Mount the fabric in a frame (see page 9) and start
each design from the centre.

If you are stitching a single design, find the
centre either by folding the fabric in half and then in
half again, and lightly pressing the folded corner, or
by marking the horizontal and vertical centre lines
with basting stitches in a light-coloured thread. For

individual designs there is no need to mount the
fabric in a hoop or frame.

Following the chart(s), complete all the cross
stitching first, using two strands of thread in the
needle. Finish with the backstitching and the french
knots, again using two strands of thread.

MOUNTING AND FRAMING

Remove the finished embroidery from the frame and
wash if necessary, then press lightly on the wrong
side, using a steam iron. If you have stitched all
designs on the same piece of fabric, cut along the
dividing lines.

For each design, spread glue evenly on one side
of the mounting card, and lightly press the batting to
the surface. Tape the embroidery over the padded
surface (see page 10), using the basting stitches (if
any) to check that the embroidery is centred over the
card. Remove basting stitches, place the mounted
embroidery in the frame, and assemble the frame
according to the manufacturer's instructions.

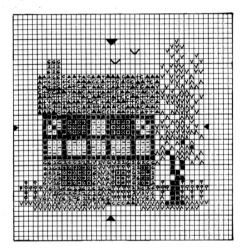

COUNTRY HOME ▲		ANCHOR	DMC	MADEIRA
•	White	1	Blanc	White
−	Light cream	386	746	101
I	Cream	885	3770	2001
9	Pale blue	130	799	1004
O	Medium blue	979	312	1005
●	Navy	127	939	1009
V	Light green	261	3363	1602
∧	Medium green	262	3051	1603
2	Light brown	369	435	2010
6	Medium brown	370	433	2008
■	Dark brown	905	3781	2106
+	Light blue grey	848	927	1708
C	Light beige	373	3046	2103
▲	Dark beige	375	420	2105
	Pink*	48	818	502

*Note: bks the window frames in white, the birds in navy, and the
base of the chimney in dark brown. Work the flowers over the door
and along the flower bed in french knots, using *pink (used for bks
only) and pale blue.*

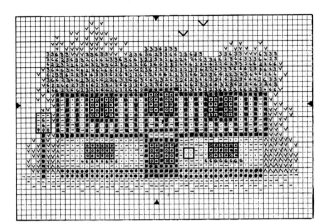

INN ▲		ANCHOR	DMC	MADEIRA
•	White	1	Blanc	White
–	Light cream	386	746	101
I	Cream	885	3770	2001
⁹	Pale blue	130	799	1004
○	Medium blue	979	312	1005
●	Navy	127	939	1009
V	Light green	261	3363	1602
∧	Medium green	262	3051	1603
2	Light brown	369	435	2010
6	Medium brown	370	433	2008
■	Dark brown	905	3781	2106
3	Dark warm brown	358	437	1910

Note: bks the window frames in white, the birds in navy, and the sign post and menu to the right of the door in dark brown. Fill window box with french knots in light green and pale blue.

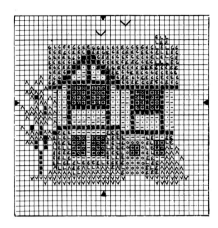

THE GABLES ▲		ANCHOR	DMC	MADEIRA
•	White	1	Blanc	White
–	Light cream	386	746	101
○	Medium blue	979	312	1005
●	Navy	127	939	1009
V	Light green	261	3363	1602
∧	Medium green	262	3051	1603
6	Medium brown	370	433	2008
■	Dark brown	905	3781	2106
+	Light blue grey	848	927	1708
L	Very light beige	372	739	1909
ε	Medium beige	374	3045	2104
▲	Dark beige	375	420	2105
	Pink*	48	818	502

Note: bks the window frames in white, the birds in navy, and the base of the chimney and lines of the wall in dark brown. Work the flowers on the bush and in the flower bed in french knots, using pink (used for bks only) and pale blue.*

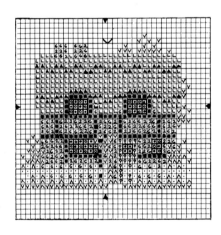

THATCHED COTTAGE ▲		ANCHOR	DMC	MADEIRA
•	White	1	Blanc	White
⁹	Pale blue	130	799	1004
○	Medium blue	979	312	1005
●	Navy	127	939	1009
V	Light green	261	3363	1602
∧	Medium green	262	3051	1603
6	Medium brown	370	433	2008
■	Dark brown	905	3781	2106
L	Very light beige	372	739	1909
	Pink*	48	818	502

Note: bks the window frames in white and the bird in navy. Work the flowers over the door and along the fence in french knots, using pink (used for bks only) and pale blue.*

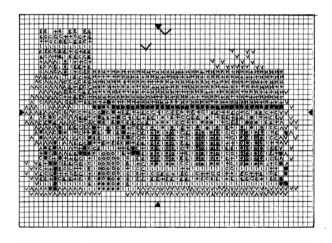

CHURCH ▲		ANCHOR	DMC	MADEIRA
I	Cream	885	3770	2001
○	Medium blue	979	312	1005
●	Navy	127	939	1009
V	Light green	261	3363	1602
∧	Medium green	262	3051	1603
■	Dark brown	905	3781	2106
+	Light blue grey	848	927	1708
H	Medium blue grey	920	932	710
C	Light beige	373	3046	2103
ε	Medium beige	374	3045	2104

Note: bks the window frames in cream, and the birds in navy.

An English Village

This charming picture shows a typical English village scene – a row of small cottages, all of differing styles and periods, nestling together amid the rural setting. It's a timeless scene that is both rewarding to stitch and display with pride in your home.

AN ENGLISH VILLAGE

YOU WILL NEED

For the English Village picture, set in a mount with a cut-out measuring 17.5cm × 7.5cm (7in × 3in):

35cm × 25cm (14in × 10in) of antique white, 14-count Aida fabric
Stranded embroidery cotton in the colours given in the appropriate panel
No 26 tapestry needle
Wooden frame, measuring 28cm × 17.5cm (11¼ × 7in)
Rectangular mount, cut to fit the frame, with cut-out as specified above
Strong thread and cardboard, for mounting

●

THE EMBROIDERY

Prepare the fabric as described on page 8; find the centre by folding, and mark the horizontal and vertical centre lines with basting stitches in a light-coloured thread. Set the fabric in a frame, and count out from the centre to start stitching at a point convenient to you.

Two threads of cotton were used in the needle for cross stitches and one for backstitch throughout these designs. Work all cross stitches first, taking them over one block of fabric and making sure that all top stitches run in the same direction. Finally, work all backstitch details.

FINISHING

Gently handwash the finished piece, if necessary, and lightly press with a steam iron on the wrong side. Stretch and mount the embroidery as explained on page 10. Insert it into the frame, behind the mount. A custom-made frame of dark wood was used for this picture, to echo the various shades of brown and gold in the cottage.

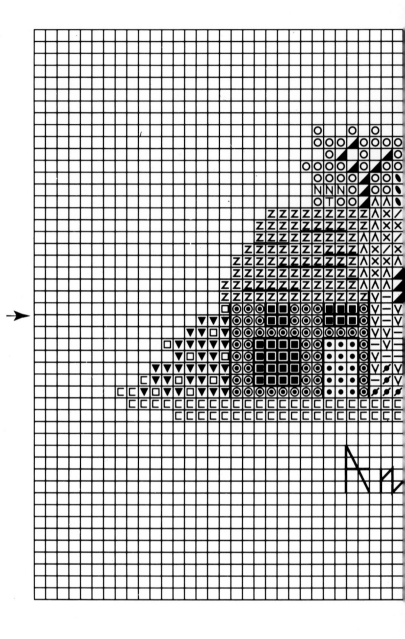

AN ENGLISH VILLAGE ▲			DMC	ANCHOR	MADEIRA
Cross	Half Cross				
T		Golden tan	420	375	2104
◤		Medium golden brown	611	889	2107
▲		Dark steel grey	646	815	1811
■		Dull grey	414	400	1801
∧		Dark drab grey	3022	393	1903
✕		Medium steel grey	647	8581	1813
╱		Light steel grey	648	900	1814
◥		Red brown	433	371	2303
⊘		Very light golden brown	613	831	2109
Ɪ		Very light grey brown	644	830	1907
◪		Light grey green	523	859	1512
V		Medium straw	3047	887	2206
—		Light straw	3046	886	2205
⅂		Soft grey blue	927	849	1708
▢		Light salmon pink	761	8	0404
◎		Light olive green	3053	216	1513

			DMC	ANCHOR	MADEIRA
Cross	Half Cross				
•		White	White	2	White
╲		Light silver grey	762	397	1804
▼		Apple green	368	261	1310
Y		Yellow	744	301	0112
⊡		Clear green	3363	861	1602
L		Very light grey green	524	858	1511
Z		Dark grey brown	640	903	1905
N		Very dark brown	839	380	1913
	⊏	Light tan	738	942	2013
◉		Light grey beige	3023	392	1903
		Dark grey*	844	401	1810

Note: bks side walls, doors and lines on left end of roof in very dark brown, window panes in white, window frames in dark grey* (used for bks only), and brickwork on house with rust roof in dark grey brown.

Church Tea Tray Set

This village church, set on a gentle hillside and surrounded by grazing sheep, is captured in soft colours on a wooden tray, with a teapot stand to match. You could also embroider individual sheep on the corners of napkins or a tablecloth.

CHURCH TEA TRAY SET

YOU WILL NEED

For the Tea Tray, measuring 32cm × 24cm
(12¾in × 9½in):

*40cm × 30cm (16in × 12in) green 14-count
Aida fabric*
*Stranded embroidery cotton in the colours given
in the panel*
No24 tapestry needle
Wooden tray (for suppliers, see page 143)

For the Teapot Stand, measuring 11.5cm
(4½in) in diameter:

*25cm × 25cm (10in × 10in) green 14-count
Aida fabric*
*Stranded embroidery cotton in the colours given
in the panel*
No24 tapestry needle
Hexagonal frame (for suppliers, see page 143)

THE EMBROIDERY

Stretch the fabric in a hoop or frame, as explained
on page 8. Following the chart, start the embroidery
at the centre of the design, using two strands of
embroidery cotton in the needle. Work each stitch
over one block of fabric in each direction. Make sure
that the top crosses run in the same direction. Gently
steam press the finished embroideries.

MAKING THE TRAY AND TEAPOT STAND

Trim the work and mount it in the tray or stand
following the manufacturer's instructions supplied
with these items.

TEA TRAY ▲		DMC	ANCHOR	MADEIRA
◩	Moss green	3012	843	1606
▽	Dark green	3051	861	1508
▣	Light green	907	255	1410
◪	Very light beige	3047	390	1908
◰	Light beige	613	831	2109
‖	Beige	744	392	0112
◬	Dark brown	801	358	2007
◉	Brown	434	944	2009
+	Light brown	3045	373	2103
▲	Dark grey	413	401	1713
▪	Blue-grey	930	922	1712
⊞	Black	310	403	Black
⊡	White	White	1	White

TEAPOT STAND ◀		DMC	ANCHOR	MADEIRA
◩	Moss green	3012	843	1606
▽	Dark green	3051	861	1508
◬	Dark brown	801	358	2007
◉	Brown	434	944	2009
⊞	Black	310	403	Black
⊡	White	White	1	White

Village School Cushion

Bowling a hoop, flying a kite,
skipping and jumping and playing
bat and ball – these all evoke
memories of school playgrounds.
With its cheerful, bright colours this
plump cushion would make a
lovely gift.

VILLAGE SCHOOL CUSHION

YOU WILL NEED

For the Village School Cushion, measuring 32cm (12³/₄in) square:

*40cm × 40cm (16in × 16in) antique white
16-count Aida fabric
Stranded embroidery cotton in the colours given
in the panel
No26 tapestry needle
40cm × 40cm (16in × 16in) medium-weight
upholstery fabric, for backing
Matching thread
35cm (14in) square cushion pad
130cm (52in) corded braid in a contrasting colour*

•

THE EMBROIDERY

Stretch the fabric in a hoop or frame, as explained on page 8. Following the chart, start the embroidery at the centre of the design, using one strand of embroidery cotton in the needle. Work each stitch over one block of fabric in each direction. Make sure that the top crosses run in the same direction. When all the cross-stitch embroidery has been worked, stitch features on the children's faces, the tennis racquet strings, and the skipping rope, using a single strand of black. Gently steam press the finished embroidery on the wrong side.

MAKING THE CUSHION

Place the completed embroidery and backing fabric with right sides together. Stitch around three sides to make a square cushion cover measuring 32cm (12³/₄in). Clip corners and trim seams, then turn right side out. Insert the cushion pad and oversew the opening in the cover. Slipstitch corded braid in place all around the edges.

VILLAGE SCHOOL CUSHION		DMC	ANCHOR	MADEIRA
∷	Skin tone	3774	1012	305
⊘	Light pink	3689	49	608
▣	Mid pink	3687	66	604
⊥	Dusty pink	3354	894	606
◲	Light mauve	554	96	0711
↓	Blue-mauve	340	109	803
♡	Brick red	920	339	401
⊟	Dark red	347	13	510
⊓	Light blue	3760	161	1012
←	Royal blue	798	131	911
⊞	Navy blue	796	941	904
⊠	Light green	703	241	1307
⊡	Turquoise green	958	186	1113
▼	Moss green	3011	845	1607
→	Yellow	445	293	110
▬	Gold	743	347	0113
●	Light brown	301	1049	2306
◉	Honey brown	437	362	2012
⊠	Brown	611	903	2107
⊞	Dark brown	801	358	2007
△	Grey	415	399	1802
▢	White	White	1	White
■	Black	310	403	Black

Note: bks features on children's faces, the tennis racquet strings, and the skipping rope in black.

Down on the Farm

The countryside is not only very beautiful, but also extremely bountiful. This matching pair of pictures, showing ploughing and the fruit harvest, celebrate the work of the country farmer.

DOWN ON THE FARM

YOU WILL NEED

For either the *Ploughing* or the *Apple Picking*
picture, each set in a frame with a centre
measuring 17.5cm × 15cm (7in × 6in):

*30cm × 27.5cm (12in × 11in) of white,
14-count Aida fabric
Stranded embroidery cotton in the colours
given in the panel
No24 tapestry needle
Picture frame, as specified above
Firm card, to fit the frame*

*Lightweight synthetic batting, the same size
as the card
Strong thread, for mounting
Glue stick*

*NOTE: one skein of each colour listed is sufficient
for both pictures.*

●

THE EMBROIDERY

Prepare the fabric as described on page 8; find the
centre either by folding the fabric in half and then in
half again, and lightly pressing the folded corner, or
by marking the horizontal and vertical centre lines
with basting stitches in a light-coloured thread.

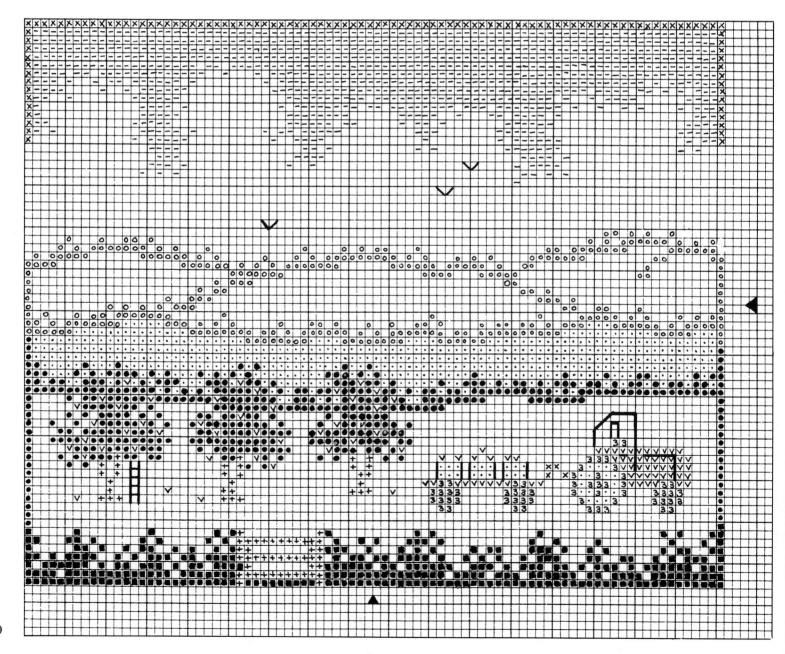

Mount the fabric in a hoop (see page 8) and start the embroidery at the centre of the design.

Following the chart, complete all the cross stitching, using two strands of thread in the needle. Finish with the backstitched details, again using two strands of thread in the needle. Be careful not to take dark threads across the back of the work in such a way that they show through on to the right side of the embroidery.

MOUNTING AND FRAMING

Remove the finished embroidery from the frame and wash if necessary, then press lightly on the wrong side, using a steam iron. Spread glue evenly on one side of the firm card, and lightly press the batting to the surface. Lace the embroidery over the padded surface (see page 10). using the basting stitches (if any) to check that the embroidery is centred over the card. Remove basting stitches, place the mounted embroidery in the frame, and assemble the frame according to the manufacturer's instructions.

DOWN ON THE FARM ▼		ANCHOR	DMC	MADEIRA
■	Dark green	245	986	1405
●	Medium green	243	988	1402
○	Light green	241	955	1210
·	Yellow	293	727	110
v	Red	13	349	212
3	Navy blue	127	939	1009
X	Medium blue	161	3760	1012
−	Pale blue	160	813	1002
+	Brown	352	300	2304

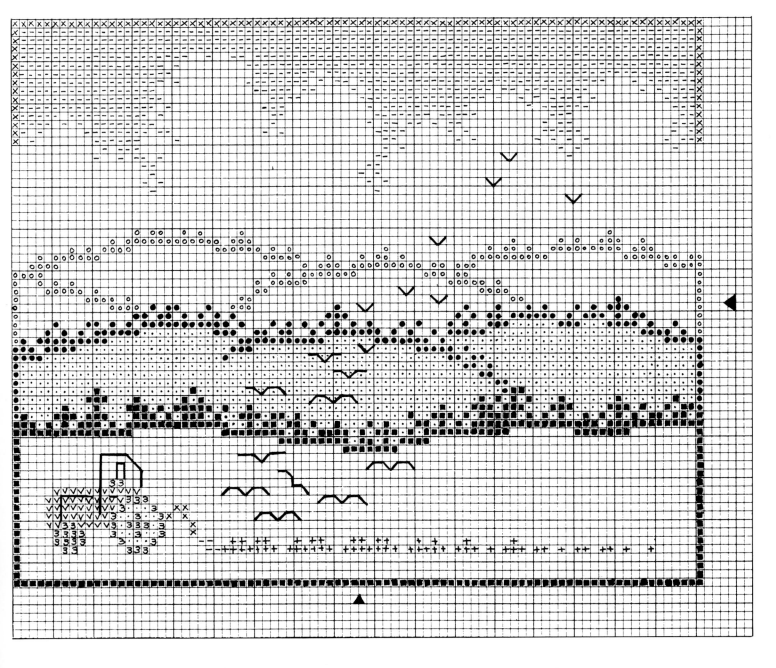

Village Grocer

Dressed neat in a white apron, this local merchant displays his wares – sacks of rice and boxes of fruit and vegetables – outside the village shop. With its straight lines and simple detail, this picture is very quick to stitch.

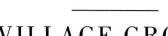

VILLAGE GROCER PICTURE

YOU WILL NEED

For the Village Grocer Picture, measuring 20cm × 13.5cm (8in × 5³⁄₈in), excluding mount:

30cm × 23.5cm (12in × 9³⁄₈in) oatmeal 14-count Aida fabric
Stranded embroidery cotton in the colours given in the panel
No24 tapestry needle
Strong thread for lacing across the back
Cardboard for mounting
Frame and mount of your choice

●

THE EMBROIDERY

Stretch the fabric in a hoop or frame, as explained on page 8. Following the chart, start the embroidery at the centre of the design, using two strands of embroidery cotton in the needle. Work each stitch over one block of fabric in each direction. Make sure that the top crosses run in the same direction. Work features on the grocer's face, the outline of his apron and the details on the sacks in black, using one strand of embroidery cotton in the needle.

MAKING UP

Gently steam press the work and mount it as explained on page 10. Lace the embroidery over the mount, following the instructions on page 10. For the best effect, display the picture behind a window mount with an aperture cut to fit the picture area exactly. Choose a frame to complement the embroidery colours: a narrow wooden frame is ideal.

VILLAGE GROCER PICTURE		DMC	ANCHOR	MADEIRA			DMC	ANCHOR	MADEIRA
⊡	White	White	1	White	⊞	Cherry red	304	47	511
▼	Black	310	403	Black	╱	Pale green	472	254	1414
△	Yellow	741	316	202	⊠	Moss green	702	256	1411
▢	Pink	604	27	413	◁	Pale blue	827	159	1002
⊡	Skin tone	950	778	2309	◁	Sea green	958	186	1113
⊞	Red	606	335	0209	⊥	Dark sea green	943	188	1203
─	Soft yellow	676	305	113	⊿	Mid blue	826	169	1012

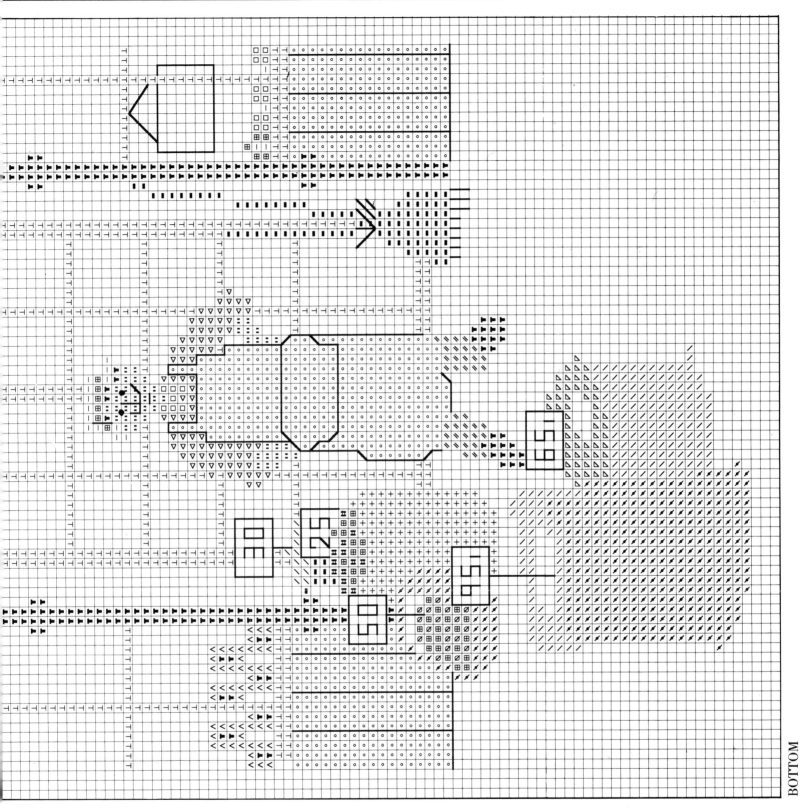

		DMC	ANCHOR	MADEIRA
☑	Beige	437	368	2011
◨	Light brown	3045	373	2103
◹	Light olive	613	956	2109
+	Tan	434	349	2306
▣	Mid olive	611	898	2107

Note: bks features on grocer's face, outline of the apron and details on the sacks in black.

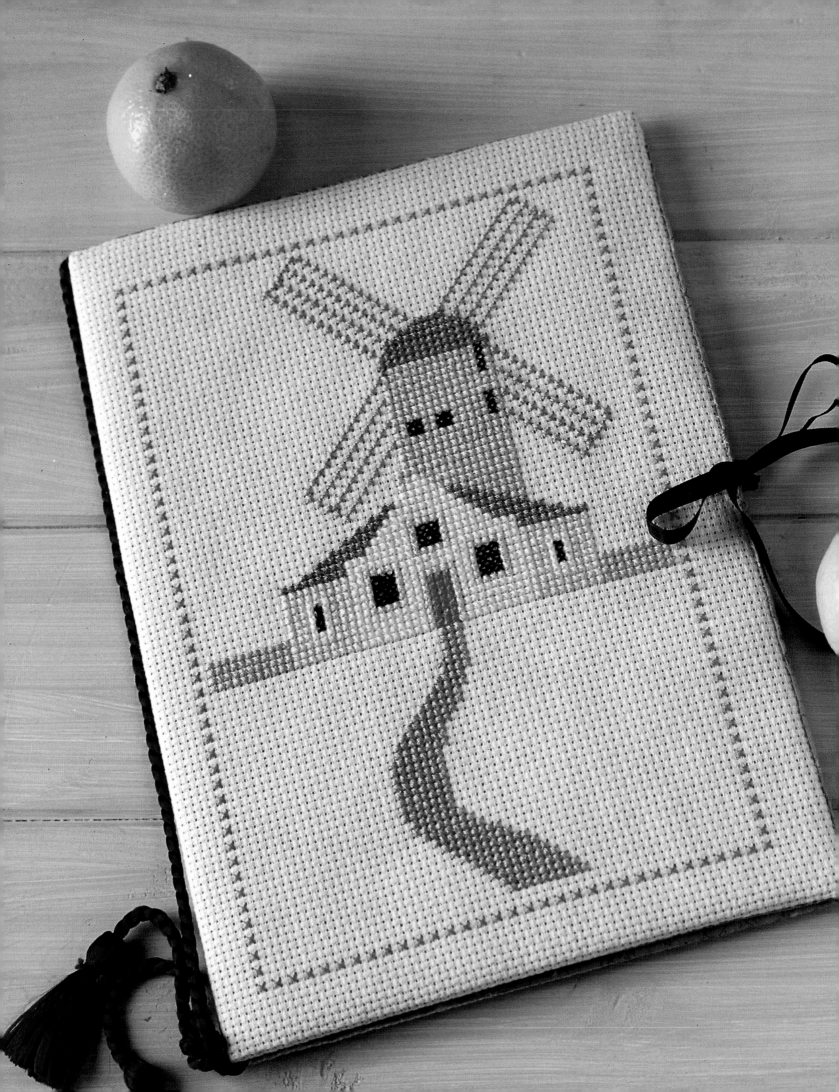

Windmill Writing Case

The clean lines of this windmill design make the project very easy to sew and ideal for beginners. On the back of the writing case is a chicken motif, which is also repeated on the greetings card.

WINDMILL
WRITING CASE

YOU WILL NEED

For the Writing Case measuring 18cm × 25cm
(7¼in × 10in) when closed:

*25cm × 32cm (10in × 12¾in) white 11-count
Aida fabric
Stranded embroidery cotton in the colours
given in the panel
No24 tapestry needle
25cm × 32cm (10in × 12¾in) polyester wadding
(batting)
Two pieces 18cm × 25cm (7¼in × 10in)
medium-weight stiff card
Fabric adhesive
25cm × 32cm (10in × 12¾in) cotton fabric,
for lining
Narrow ribbon and tasselled cord, to decorate*

For the Greetings Card, measuring 14cm × 9.5cm
(5½in × 3¾in), with an oval portrait cut-out
measuring 8.5cm × 6.5cm (3⅜in × 2½in):

*10cm × 12cm (4in × 4¾in) white 11-count
Aida fabric
Stranded embroidery cotton in the colours given in
the panel
No24 tapestry needle
Greetings card (for suppliers see page 143)
Fabric adhesive*

●

THE EMBROIDERY

Stretch the fabric in a hoop or frame, as explained
on page 8. Following the chart, start the embroidery
at the centre of the design, using two strands of
embroidery cotton in the needle. Work each stitch
over one block of fabric in each direction. Make sure
that the top crosses run in the same direction. Gently
steam press the finished embroideries.

MAKING THE WRITING CASE

Lay the embroidery face-down on a flat work surface. Place the wadding (batting) on top. Lay the two
pieces of card centrally on top, leaving a gap of 2cm
(¾in) in the centre, to form the spine. Trim the
wadding (batting) to the same size as the card, then

fold over the raw edges of the Aida fabric and glue
them to the card with fabric adhesive. Fold in the
edges of the lining fabric, so that the fabric fits the
inside of the writing case exactly. Place the fabric on
top to hide the glued edges. Insert two ribbon ties in
the centres of the long edges, then oversew all
around using small, neat stitches and catching in the
ribbon as you go. Knot the tasselled cord and slip it
over one of the short edges, positioning it on the
spine of the writing case.

MAKING THE GREETINGS CARD

Trim the embroidery fabric to fit the inside of the
card. Position the embroidery centrally behind the
cut-out, then fold over the front flap of the card and
glue it in place with fabric adhesive.

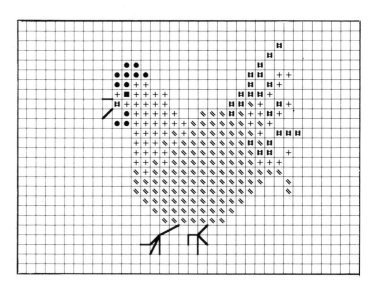

CHICKEN ▲		DMC	ANCHOR	MADEIRA
●	Black	310	403	Black
⊠	Red	892	35	412
⊞	Golden yellow	437	891	2012
⊞	Light brown	3064	882	2312
■	Pale brick	356	338	402

Note: bks chicken's beak and feet in orange.

WINDMILL ▶		DMC	ANCHOR	MADEIRA
■	Black	310	403	Black
●	Red	892	35	412
⊡	Pink	353	8	304
○	Yellow	726	295	109
⊠	Golden yellow	437	891	2012
✳	Green-grey	926	850	1707
↑	Golden olive	3046	887	2206
⊥	Grey	452	232	1807
⊞	Light brown	3064	882	2312
⊞	Pale brick	356	338	402

Maypole Tea Cosy

This joyful scene depicts the children of the village dancing around a maypole. Make it up into a tea cosy, as here, or frame the finished work to make a picture for the nursery wall.

MAYPOLE TEA COSY

and stitch along three sides, to the same measurements as the outer part of the tea cosy and leaving one side open. Trim seams. Cut two pieces of wadding (batting) to the same size and shape as the tea cosy. Place inside the tea cosy, then insert the lining. Starting with the bottom opening, bind all raw edges. To make a looped handle at the top, cover the piping cord with a length of bias binding and stitch in place. Sew ribbon roses on either side, to hide the join.

YOU WILL NEED

For the Maypole Tea Cosy, measuring 28cm × 26cm (11¼in × 10⅜in):

30cm × 30cm (12in × 12in) sage green 14-count Aida fabric
Stranded embroidery cotton in the colours given in the panel
No24 tapestry needle
Matching thread
28cm × 26cm (11¼in × 10⅜in) plain or patterned cotton furnishing fabric, for backing
30cm × 60cm (12in × 24in) soft cotton fabric, for lining
30cm × 60cm (12in × 24in) medium-weight polyester wadding (batting)
1.5m (60in) of 2.5cm (1in) bias binding, in a contrasting colour
10cm (4in) length of piping cord
Ribbon roses, to decorate

•

THE EMBROIDERY

Stretch the fabric in a hoop or frame, as explained on page 8. Following the chart, start the embroidery at the centre of the design, using two strands of embroidery cotton in the needle. Work each stitch over one block of fabric in each direction. Make sure that the top crosses run in the same direction. Work features on the children's faces in black, using one strand of embroidery cotton in the needle. Gently steam press the finished embroidery on the wrong side.

MAKING UP THE TEA COSY

Trim the finished embroidery to 28cm × 26cm (11¼in × 10⅜in) and baste to the backing fabric. Cut the top corners to a smooth, rounded shape.

Fold the lining fabric in half, right sides together,

MAYPOLE TEA COSY ▶	DMC	ANCHOR	MADEIRA
○ White	White	1	White
▲ Black	310	403	Black
⊡ Bright blue	798	146	911
⊥ Lilac	340	118	902
◇ Pink	224	893	404
↓ Pinky-purple	3608	86	709
← Pale blue	3755	130	907
▽ Yellow	726	305	113
△ Mid steel	415	399	1802
⊘ Pale flesh	951	1011	306
◉ Aqua blue	3761	9159	1014
⊘ Mid purple	209	109	803
◰ Brown	3781	358	2008
→ Red	3705	35	412
↑ Leaf green	703	238	1307
⊠ Dark purple	333	119	903
⊡ Pale grey	3072	397	1901
▽ Blue	799	131	911
⊟ Orange	742	306	0114
⊓ Mid tan brown	783	901	2210
◪ Rich dark brown	801	359	2007
◹ Khaki	372	854	2110
✳ Pale blue-grey	928	274	1709
⊐ Skin tone	754	1012	305
▣ Purple	208	110	804
◁ Pale green	3348	254	1409

Note: bks features on artist's face in black, and steps in brown.

SEASONS IN THE COUNTRY

The distinctive characteristics and particular charm of each of the four seasons are displayed in the projects on the following pages. Starting with spring, daffodils, violets, delicate primroses and a spring bunny – all of these evoke the freshest of the seasons, with its promise of new life.

PROMISE OF SPRING

YOU WILL NEED

For the *Spring* picture, set in a mount with a cut-out measuring 12.5cm × 16cm (5in × 6¼in):

32.5cm × 36cm, (13in × 14¼in) of antique white, 18-count Aida fabric
Stranded embroidery cotton in the colours given in the panel
No26 tapestry needle
Wooden frame measuring 22.5cm × 26cm (8¾in × 10¼in)
Rectangular mount, cut to fit the frame, with cut-out as specified above
Strong thread and cardboard, for mounting

●

THE EMBROIDERY

Prepare the fabric as described on page 8; find the centre by folding and mark the horizontal and vertical centre lines with basting stitches in a light-coloured thread. Set the fabric in a frame or hoop (see page 9) and count out from the centre to start stitching at a point convenient to you.

One thread of cotton was used in the needle for cross stitches and for backstitch. Work all full cross stitches first, and then the half crosses. The half cross stitches have their own individual symbols on the chart; for each half cross, work only the top stitch of the two that make up a full cross stitch, to produce a more delicate effect.

Take both half and full crosses over one block of the fabric, making sure that all top stitches run in the same direction (if top stitches run in different directions, they will reflect the light in opposite directions and the work will look uneven). Finally, work all backstitch details.

FINISHING

Gently handwash the finished piece, if necessary, and lightly press with a steam iron on the wrong side. Stretch and mount the embroidery as explained on page 10. Insert it into the frame, behind the rectangular mount.

For each of these seasonal pictures, the colour of the mount has been specially selected to echo colours and tones predominant in that particular design, but if you are making them as a set, you might prefer to use one colour for all four.

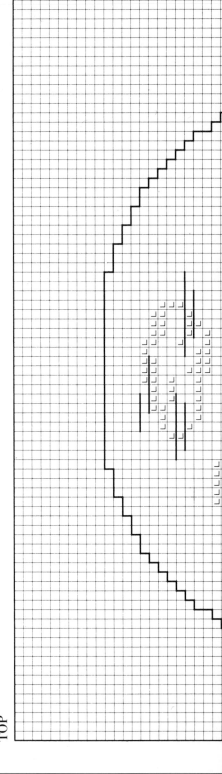

TOP

PROMISE OF SPRING ▲			DMC	ANCHOR	MADEIRA
Cross	Half Cross				
•		Very light mauve	3743	869	0801
O		Light antique mauve	3042	870	0807
▲		Medium antique mauve	3041	871	0806
X		Medium yellow	744	301	0112
S		Medium grey-green	522	860	1513
V	/	Very light grey-green	524	858	1511
–		Light yellow	745	300	0111
△		Medium gold	725	305	0108
■		Light orange	402	1047	2307

BOTTOM

Cross	Half Cross		DMC	ANCHOR	MADEIRA
●		Medium brownish green	3052	859	1509
C		Light yellow green	3364	266	1501
		Dark golden brown*	611	898	2107
B		Medium golden brown	612	832	2108
T		Light golden brown	613	831	2109
P		Pale shell pink	3713	48	0502
	I	Light grass green	471	266	1501
U		White	White	2	White
M		Pale cream	822	390	1908

Cross	Half Cross		DMC	ANCHOR	MADEIRA
		Medium khaki*	370	855	2112
\		Light khaki	372	853	2110
		Medium cornflower blue*	794	175	0907
L		Very light cornflower blue	3747	120	1002

Note: backstitch the border outline in medium khaki, the violets and bunny in dark brown* and the lines on the sky in medium cornflower blue* (starred outline colours are not indicated by symbols on the chart). The bunny's eye is stitched with a half cross in dark golden brown**

A Touch of Summer

The summer garden is a riot of colour
and fragrance, attracting natural
visitors, such as brightly-coloured
butterflies; the summer flowers and
fruit at the front of this design lead
the eye to the view of a cottage
garden behind, complete with a
rose-covered arch.

A TOUCH OF SUMMER

YOU WILL NEED

For the *Summer* picture, set in a mount with a cut-out measuring 12.5cm × 16cm (5in × 6¼in):

32.5cm × 36cm (13in × 14¼in) of antique white, 18-count Aida fabric
Stranded embroidery cotton in the colours given in the panel
No26 tapestry needle
Wooden frame measuring 22.5cm × 26cm (8¾in × 10¼in)
Rectangular mount, cut to fit the frame, with cut-out as specified above
Strong thread and cardboard, for mounting

•

THE EMBROIDERY

Prepare the fabric as described on page 8; find the centre by folding, and mark the horizontal and vertical centre lines with basting stitches in a light-coloured thread. Set the fabric in a frame or hoop

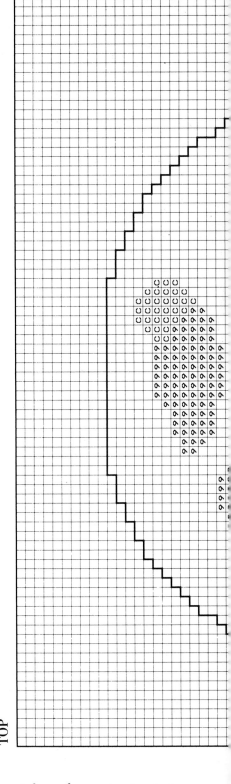

TOP

A TOUCH OF SUMMER ▶			DMC	ANCHOR	MADEIRA
Cross	**Half Cross**				
•		White	White	2	White
−		Very light pink	819	271	0501
O		Pale shell pink	3713	48	0502
P		Light salmon pink	761	8	0404
▲		Medium salmon pink	760	9	0405
Y		Medium yellow	744	301	0112
C		Light yellow	745	300	0111
B	/	Light golden brown	613	831	2109
		Dark golden brown*	611	898	2107
●		Clear green	3363	262	1602
L		Medium grey green	522	860	1513
V	\	Very light grey green	524	858	1511
S		Light khaki	372	853	2110
■		Medium olive green	3052	859	1509
R		Light olive green	3053	844	1510
6		Light cornflower blue	794	175	0907
△		Medium cornflower blue	793	176	0906
X		Apple green	368	240	1310
8		Medium khaki	370	855	2112
U		Light grass green	471	253	1414
=		Dark pink	3712	1023	0406
⁄⁄		Light orange	402	1047	2307
♥		Dark golden brown	611	898	2107
	9	Very pale blue	3753	1031	1001
		Dark grey*	646	815	1809

Note: backstitch the border outline in clear green, fence in dark grey, and strawberry flowers, daisies and butterfly in dark golden brown* (starred outline colours are not indicated by symbols on the chart). Using dark golden brown, make either tiny stitches or french knots to form the dots in the wings and feelers of the butterfly.*

(see page 9) and count out from the centre to start stitching at a point convenient to you.

One thread of cotton was used in the needle for cross stitches and for backstitch. Work all full cross stitches first, and then the half crosses. The half cross stitches have their own individual symbols on the chart; for each half cross, work only the top stitch of the two that make up a full cross stitch, to produce a more delicate effect.

Take both half and full crosses over one block of

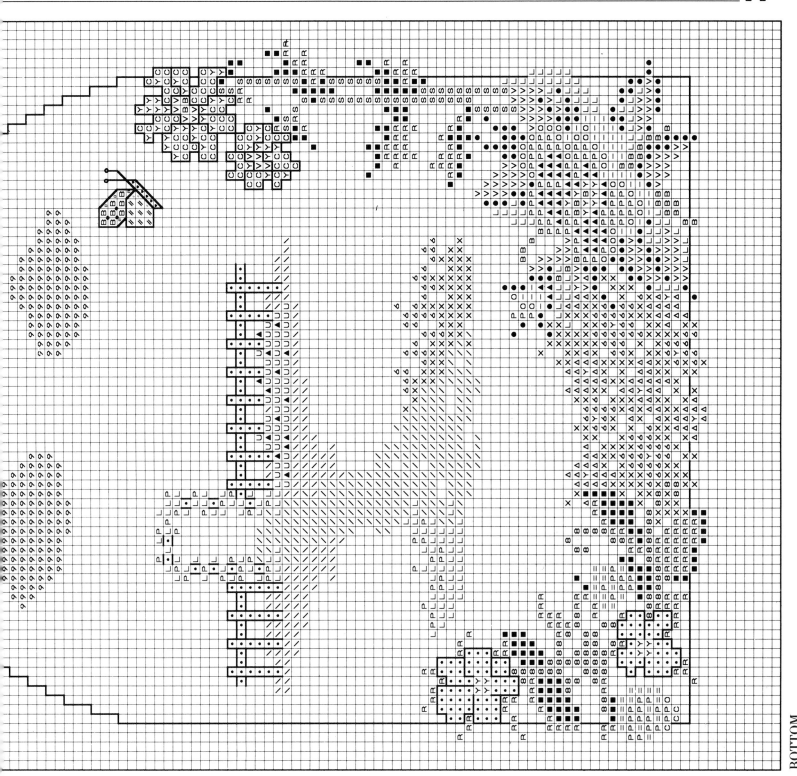

BOTTOM

the fabric, making sure that all top stitches run in the same direction (if top stitches run in different directions, they will reflect the light in opposite directions and the work will look uneven). Finally, work all backstitch details.

FINISHING

Gently handwash the finished piece, if necessary, and lightly press with a steam iron on the wrong side. Stretch and mount the embroidery as explained on page 10. Insert it into the frame, behind the rectangular mount.

For each of these seasonal pictures, the colour of the mount has been specially selected to echo colours and tones predominant in that particular design, but if you are making them as a set, you might prefer to use one colour for all four.

Autumn Harvest Tray

The fruits of autumn in all their abundance and rich colourings are vividly portrayed on this stitched piece, which has been made up in the form of a tray. Used throughout the year, it reminds us of earth's bounty and blessings.

AUTUMN HARVEST TRAY

For the tray, measuring 24cm (9½in) square:

37.5cm (15in) square of 14-count,
Fiddler's Lite Aida fabric
Stranded embroidery cotton in the colours
given in the panel
No24 tapestry needle
Wooden tray (for suppliers, see page 143)

●

THE EMBROIDERY

Prepare the fabric as described on page 8; find the centre by folding, and mark the horizontal and vertical centre lines with basting stitches in a light-coloured thread. Set the fabric in a frame or hoop and count out from the centre to start stitching at a point convenient to you.

Two threads of cotton were used in the needle for cross stitches and one for backstitching. Work all cross stitches first, taking them over one block of fabric. Make sure that all top stitches run in the same direction. Finally, work all backstitch details.

Remove the embroidery from the frame, and, if necessary, wash gently and then steam press on the wrong side. Do not remove the basting stitches at this stage.

ASSEMBLING THE TRAY

Using a soft pencil, mark the mounting card supplied with the tray horizontally and vertically across the centre. Place the embroidery face down with the card on top, basting and pencil lines matching.

Fold the fabric over at each corner, securing it with masking tape. Working on one side and then the opposite side, fold over the edges of the fabric on all sides and secure with pieces of masking tape. Check to see that the embroidery is centred; if not, simply release the masking tape and readjust the position. Neaten the corners by folding them over to form a mitre and secure with masking tape. Carefully remove basting stitches.

Insert the mounted embroidery into the tray, using the glass and backing boards provided and following the manufacturer's instructions.

AUTUMN HARVEST ▶		DMC	ANCHOR	MADEIRA
X	Light grey green	523	859	1512
●	Pink red	3328	1024	0406
P	Medium salmon pink	760	9	0405
╱	Light salmon pink	761	8	0404
G	Clear green	3363	262	1602
	Dark tan brown*	433	359	2304
O	Medium tan brown	435	371	2303
T	Light tan brown	437	362	2012
L	Medium gold	676	891	2208
M	Medium purple	553	98	0712
─	Light purple	554	96	0711
▲	Dark yellow green	3051	681	1508
I	Light straw	3047	852	2205
S	Medium straw	3046	887	2206
U	Khaki green	370	855	2112
A	Apple green	368	261	1310
B	Medium golden brown	612	832	2108
C	Medium orange	722	323	0307
╲	Light orange	402	1047	2307
Y	Medium yellow	744	301	0112
•	Light gold	677	886	2205
■	Dark tan	420	374	2104

Note: backstitch the basket outline, the fruit stems and wheatsheaf in dark tan brown (used for backstitch only) and the outer line and flourishes in clear green.*

Autumn Glories

Everywhere in this design there is evidence of the earth's rich abundance and the harvest at the end of the year. Vivid autumnal colours offset the darkening sky, with migrating birds etched against the clouds.

AUTUMN GLORIES

YOU WILL NEED

For the *Autumn* picture, set in a mount with a cut-out measuring 12.5cm × 16cm (5in × 6¼in):

32.5cm × 36cm (13in × 14¼in) of antique white, 18-count Aida fabric
Stranded embroidery cotton in the colours given in the appropriate panel
No26 tapestry needle
Wooden frame measuring 22.5cm × 26cm (8¾in × 10¼in)
Rectangular mount, cut to fit the frame, with cut-out as specified above
Strong thread and cardboard, for mounting

•

THE EMBROIDERY

Prepare the fabric as described on page 8; find the centre by folding, and mark the horizontal and vertical centre lines with basting stitches in a light-coloured thread. Set the fabric in a frame or hoop (see page 9) and count out from the centre to start stitching at a point convenient to you.

One thread of cotton was used in the needle for cross stitches and for backstitch. Work all full cross stitches first, and then the half crosses. The half cross stitches have their own individual symbols on the chart; for each half cross, work only the top stitch of the two that make up a full cross stitch, to produce a more delicate effect.

Take both half and full crosses over one block of the fabric, making sure that all top stitches run in the same direction (if top stitches run in different directions, they will reflect the light in opposite directions and the work will look uneven). Finally, work all backstitch details.

FINISHING

Gently handwash the finished piece, if necessary, and lightly press with a steam iron on the wrong side. Stretch and mount the embroidery as explained on page 10. Insert it into the frame, behind the rectangular mount.

For each of these seasonal pictures, the colour of the mount has been specially selected to echo colours and tones predominant in that particular design, but if you are making them as a set, you might prefer to use one colour for all four.

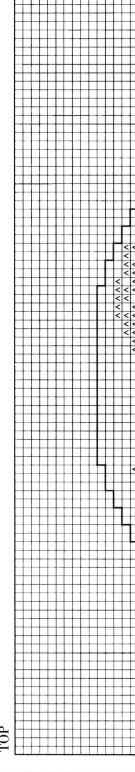

TOP

AUTUMN GLORIES ▲			DMC	ANCHOR	MADEIRA
Cross	Half Cross				
O	I	Light yellow green	3364	266	1501
Y		Medium yellow	744	301	0112
▲	▲	Light gold	725	305	0108
B		Medium golden brown	612	832	2108
L	\	Light golden brown	613	831	2109
R		Dark peach red	350	11	0213
=		Medium peach red	351	10	0214
S		Medium khaki	370	855	2112

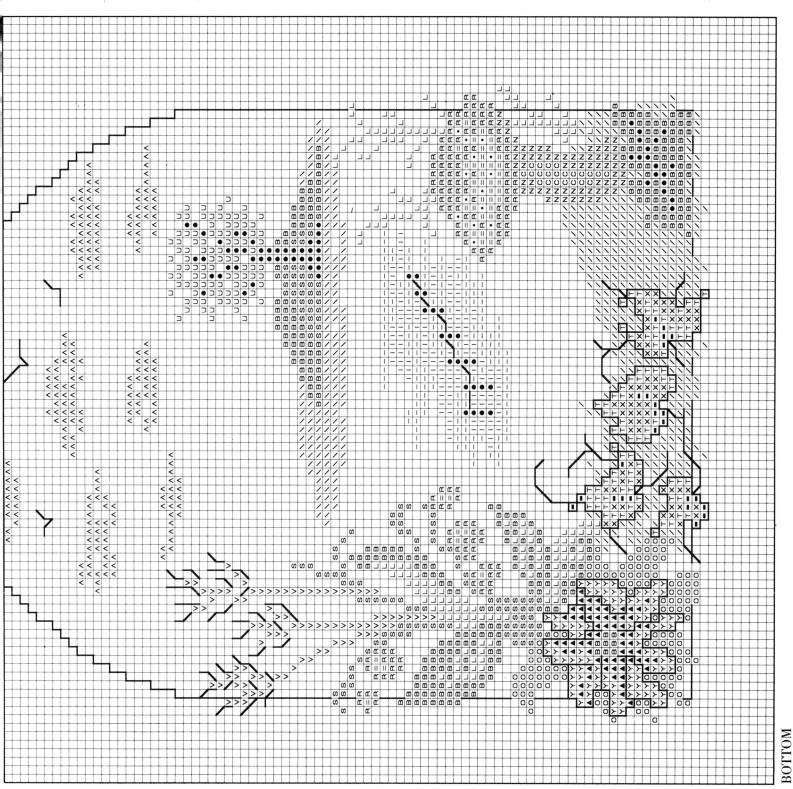

BOTTOM

Cross	Half Cross		DMC	ANCHOR	MADEIRA
V	/	Light khaki	372	853	2110
■		Dark brown	869	944	2105
T		Medium golden tan	420	374	2104
X		Light tan	680	901	2210
•		White	White	2	White
C		Light brown grey	3024	397	1901
N		Medium brown grey	3023	899	1902
●		Dark golden brown	611	898	2107

Cross	Half Cross		DMC	ANCHOR	MADEIRA
U		Light orange	402	1047	2307
	Λ	Very light grey blue	928	900	1709
	−	Pale gold	677	886	2205

Note: backstitch the border outline in medium golden tan, and the grasses, ivy leaves, chrysanthemums, fence and bird outlines in dark golden brown.

Winter Landscape Cards

Winter is a time with its own stark beauty. These two delicate landscape pictures, designed to evoke the wintry scene, have been stitched as cards, but they would also make an appealing pair of small pictures.

WINTER LANDSCAPE CARDS

For each card, start by preparing the fabric as described on page 8; find the centre by folding, and mark the horizontal and vertical centre lines with basting stitches in a light-coloured thread. Set the fabric in a hoop (see page 9) and count out from the centre to start stitching at a point convenient to you. Use two strands of embroidery cotton in the needle for both cross stitches and half cross stitches, and take each stitch over two threads of the linen fabric. Finish with the backstitching, using one strand of embroidery cotton in the needle.

YOU WILL NEED

For each card, measuring 20.5cm × 15cm (8in × 6in), with a cut-out measuring 14cm × 10cm (5½in × 4in):

23cm × 17.5cm (9in × 7in) of grey, 28-count Jubilee linen fabric
Stranded embroidery cotton in the colours given in the panel
No24 tapestry needle
Masking tape
Card with cut-out as specified above (available from many needlework and craft shops; see also suppliers listed on page 143)

NOTE: if you cannot obtain Jubilee linen, substitute any other 28-count linen fabric, or use 14-count Aida; if you are stitching both pictures, you will only require one skein of each of the colours listed.

FINISHING

Remove the basting stitches. Gently handwash the finished embroidery, if necessary, and press lightly on the wrong side. Carefully trim the linen, leaving it approximately 2.5cm (1in) larger than the cut-out each way, and making sure that the design remains centred. Position the embroidery behind the aperture and use masking tape to secure it in place (some cards are self-sealing, in which case you will not require masking tape).

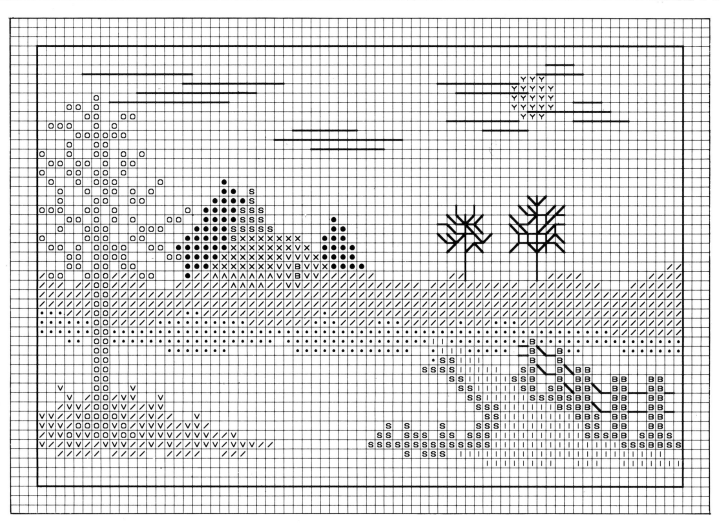

WINTER SUN ▲

Cross	Half Cross		DMC	ANCHOR	MADEIRA
O		Dark grey brown	640	903	1903
	/	Light grey	415	398	1803
V		Light golden brown	613	831	2109
	•	Very light grey	762	397	1804
●		Dark green	520	862	1514
S		Clear green	3363	262	1602
B		Dark golden brown	611	898	2107
Λ	I	Light brown grey	3023	899	1902
Y		Pale gold	677	882	2205
X		Dark tan brown	433	371	2008
		Dark grey*	414	235	1801
		Very dark golden brown*	610	905	1914
		Light blue grey*	927	849	1708

Note: backstitch the border in dark grey; the trees and fence links in very dark golden brown*, and the lines on the sky in light blue grey* (starred colours are used for backstitch only).*

WINTER LAKE ◄

Cross	Half Cross		DMC	ANCHOR	MADEIRA
	I	Light brown grey	3023	899	1902
	X	Medium brown grey	3022	392	1903
S		Clear green	3363	262	1602
●		Dark grey	520	862	1514
	/	Light grey	415	398	1803
	•	Very light grey	762	397	1804
R		Light red	3328	1024	0406
V		Medium grey green	522	860	1513
	\	Light golden brown	613	831	2109
	L	Light blue grey	927	848	1708
		Dark grey*	414	235	1801
		Very dark golden brown*	610	905	1914

Note: backstitch the sky in light blue grey; the border in dark grey, and the trees in very dark golden brown* (starred colours are used for backstitch only).*

Winter Blessings

In the foreground of this design, the delicate fragility of a Christmas rose and snowdrops is offset by the brilliance of holly berries. In the background is a cherry robin, and a wintry view of snow-covered hills.

WINTER BLESSINGS

YOU WILL NEED

For the *Winter* picture, set in a mount with a cut-out measuring 12.5cm × 16cm (5in × 6¼in):

32.5cm × 36cm (13in × 14¼in) of antique white, 18-count Aida fabric
Stranded embroidery cotton in the colours given in the panel
No26 tapestry needle
Wooden frame measuring 22.5cm × 26cm (8¾in × 10¼in)
Rectangular mount, cut to fit the frame, with cut-out as specified above
Strong thread and cardboard, for mounting

•

THE EMBROIDERY

Prepare the fabric as described on page 8; find the centre by folding, and mark the horizontal and vertical centre lines with basting stitches in a light-coloured thread. Set the fabric in a frame or hoop (see page 9) and count out from the centre to start stitching at a point convenient to you.

One thread of cotton was used in the needle for cross stitches and for backstitch. Work all full cross stitches first, and then the half crosses. The half cross stitches have their own individual symbols on the chart; for each half cross, work only the top stitch of the two that make up a full cross stitch, to produce a more delicate effect.

Take both half and full crosses over one block of the fabric, making sure that all top stitches run in the same direction (if top stitches run in different directions, they will reflect the light in opposite directions and the work will look uneven). Finally, work all backstitch details.

FINISHING

Gently handwash the finished piece, if necessary, and lightly press with a steam iron on the wrong side. Stretch and mount the embroidery as explained on page 10. Insert it into the frame, behind the rectangular mount.

For each of these seasonal pictures, the colour of the mount has been specially selected to echo colours and tones predominant in that particular design, but if you are making them as a set, you might prefer to use one colour for all four.

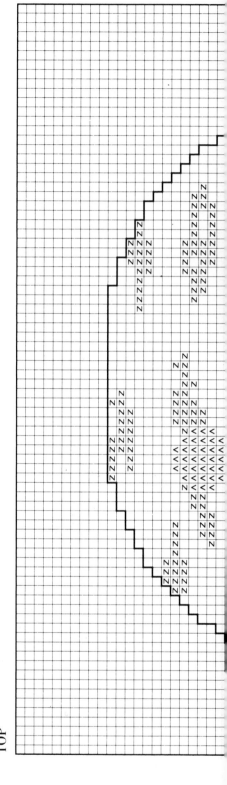

TOP

WINTER BLESSINGS ▲		DMC	ANCHOR	MADEIRA
Cross Half Cross				
●	Dark blue green	501	878	1704
X	Medium blue green	502	876	1703
V	Light blue green	503	875	1702
B	Dark golden brown	611	898	2107
▪	Dark red	349	13	0212
R	Peach red	350	11	0213
·	White	White	2	White
/	Pale cream	712	926	2101
△	Dark olive green	3051	681	1508

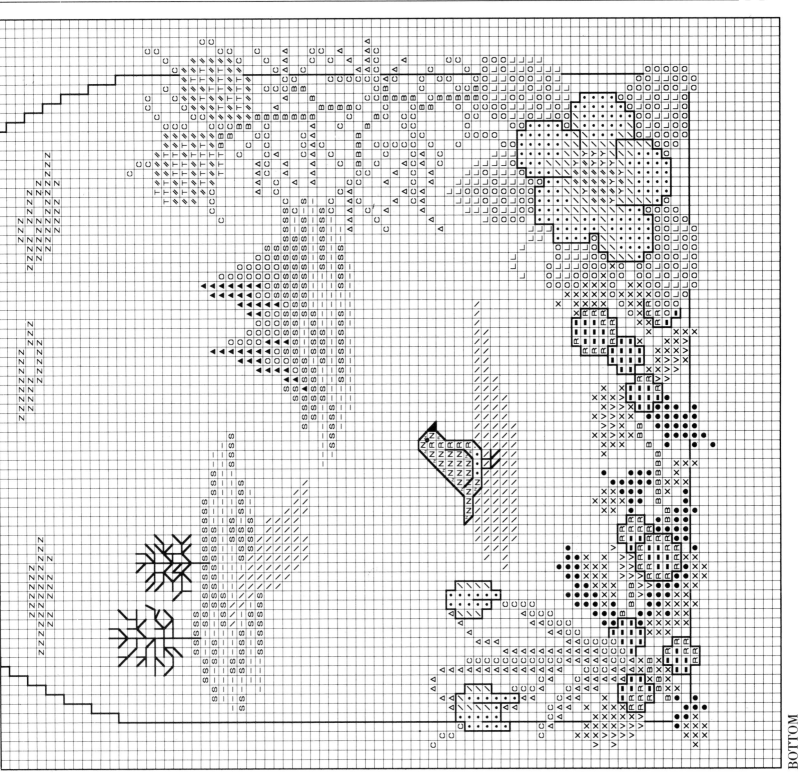

	DMC	ANCHOR	MADEIRA			DMC	ANCHOR	MADEIRA
Cross Half Cross					**Cross Half Cross**			
C	Light yellow green	3364	266	1501	\	Light golden brown	613	831	2109
O	Clear green	3363	262	1602	N	Medium grey brown	640	903	1905
L	Light grey green	523	859	1512	Λ	Pale gold	677	882	2205
⁄	Medium golden brown	612	832	2108	Z	Pale steel grey	647	1040	1813
Y	Medium yellow	744	301	0112					
T	Medium golden tan	420	374	2104					
▲	Dark fir green	520	862	1514					
S	Light grey	415	398	1803					
−	Very light grey	762	397	1804					

Note: backstitch snowdrops in light yellow green, border outline and Christmas rose in dark grey*, and robin, berries and distant trees in dark golden brown* (starred outline colours are used for backstitch only).

FLOWERS AND WOODLANDS

The enchanting wild flowers and woodlands of the countryside are featured in the projects on the following pages. Shown here, equally suitable for a living room or bedroom, this charming and delicate cushion will bring the beauty of wild flowers into your home even in the depths of winter.

WILD FLOWER CUSHION

YOU WILL NEED

For the cushion cover, measuring
30cm (12in) square:

40cm (16in) square of pink, 14-count Aida fabric
40cm (16in) square of pink cotton fabric,
for the cover back
Stranded embroidery cotton in the colours
given in the panel
No26 tapestry needle
1.3m (1½yds) of green cord, for trimming
Matching pink and green sewing cotton
Cushion pad (for a plump effect, choose a cushion
pad slightly larger than the measurements of
the finished cover)

●

THE EMBROIDERY

Prepare the fabric as described on page 8; find the centre either by folding the fabric in half and then in half again, and lightly pressing the folded corner, or by marking the horizontal and vertical centre lines with basting stitches in a light-coloured thread. Mount the fabric in a frame (see page 9) and count out from the centre to start at an appropriate point.

Following the chart, complete all the cross stitching, using two strands of thread in the needle. Be careful not to take dark threads across the back of the work in such a way that they show through on the right side.

MAKING THE COVER

Remove the finished embroidery from the frame and wash if necessary, then press lightly on the wrong side, using a steam iron. Keeping the embroidery centred, trim the embroidery fabric to measure 32.5cm (13in) square. Place the embroidery and backing fabric with right sides together and machine stitch around the edges, taking a 12mm (÷™in) seam allowance and leaving a 25cm (10in) gap at one side edge.

Trim across the seam allowance at the corners, to remove excess fabric, and turn the cover right side out. Insert the cushion pad into the cover, fold in the remaining seam allowances and slipstitch the opening, leaving a small gap at one end for the cord

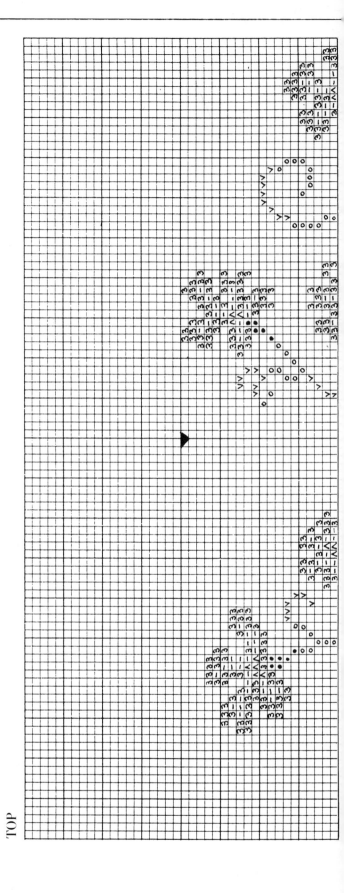

ends. Pin the cord trim around the edge of the cushion cover, tucking one end into the opening. Neatly slipstitch the cord in place, tucking the remaining end into the opening when you reach the starting point again, and stitching across the opening to seal it.

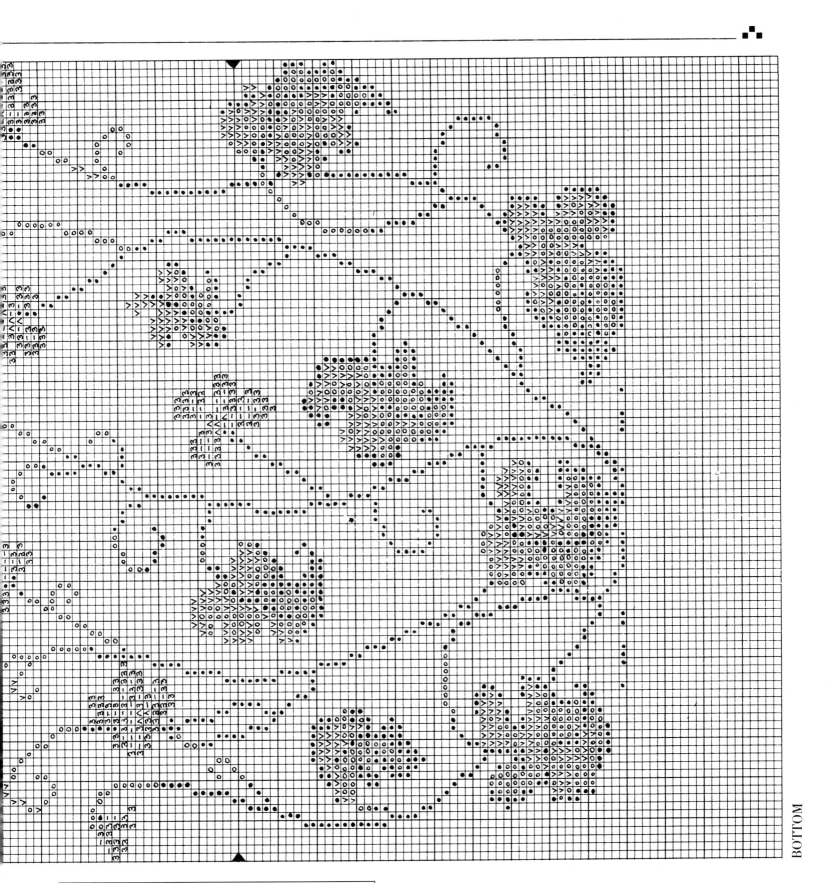

WILD FLOWER ▲			
CUSHION	ANCHOR	DMC	MADEIRA
• Light green	261	3363	1602
O Medium green	262	3364	1603
V Dark green	263	935	1505
− Lilac	98	553	712
3 Purple	101	552	713
∧ Yellow	306	725	113

Daisy Patch Tablecloth

A fresh sprinkling of daisies lies in a
diagonal pattern across this charming
tablecloth, which would be ideal for
lunch or tea on the lawn on a
summer's day. If you choose, you
might embroider the daisy motifs
on a matching set of napkins.

DAISY PATCH
TABLECLOTH

YOU WILL NEED

For the tablecloth, measuring
approximately 162cm (64in) square:

*1.75m (2yds) of Zweigart Favourite, 2215
(for suppliers, see page 143)
6m (6²⁄₃yds) of lace trim,
approximately 12mm (¹⁄₂in) deep
Stranded embroidery cotton in the colours given in
the panel; you will require one skein of orange and
three skeins of each of the other colours listed
No24 tapestry needle*

●

THE EMBROIDERY

Trim the cloth to make it a square, then either
overlock the edges by machine and turn and stitch a
4cm (1¹⁄₂in) hem or make a 12mm (¹⁄₂in) fold and
then a 2.5cm (1in) fold and handsew the hem. Pin
and stitch the lace trim in position along the folded
edge.

As can be seen in the diagram, the pattern runs
diagonally across the cloth, diagonal rows of daisy
patches, one to each Aida circle, alternating with
diagonal rows of single daisies. In order that the
cloth looks the same from the opposite sides, the
motifs are alternately stitched facing the right way
up, and then flipped vertically in the next circle to
face upside down.

It is important to use a hoop for this project (see
page 8), as the weave of the fabric is loose and the
stitching would otherwise deform the Aida circles.
Never leave your work in the hoop when you are not
stitching, as this can leave marks on the cloth.

Use three strands of thread in the needle for both
the cross stitching and the backstitched flower
stalks. Be careful not to take dark threads across the
back of the work in such a way that they show
through on the right side. It is also important to
ensure that threads are fastened securely, as the
tablecloth will need to withstand the rigours of
constant use and washing.

NAPKINS

If you wish to make a set of table napkins to match
your cloth, you can either use the same fabric,
allowing approximately a 45cm (17in) square of

fabric for each napkin, or purchase ready-prepared
napkins from the suppliers listed on page 143.

Choose your motif (you might decide to set the
single flower at one corner and the patch of daisies
at the opposite corner of each napkin). Work out how
far from the edge you wish to set each motif, then
count up an even number of threads from each side
of the corner and baste guidelines along each edge,
crossing at the corner, to help to ensure that the
motif is correctly positioned.

THE DAISY PATCH ▶	ANCHOR	DMC	MADEIRA
☐ Light blue	131	798	911
● Dark blue	132	797	912
V Light green	243	988	1402
∧ Dark green	245	986	1405
▬ Orange	314	741	201

Note: bks flower stalks in dark green.

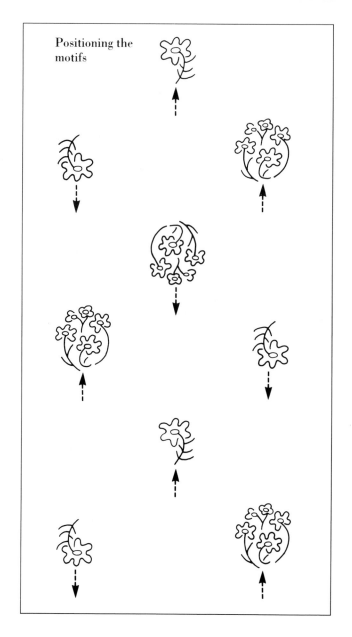

Positioning the
motifs

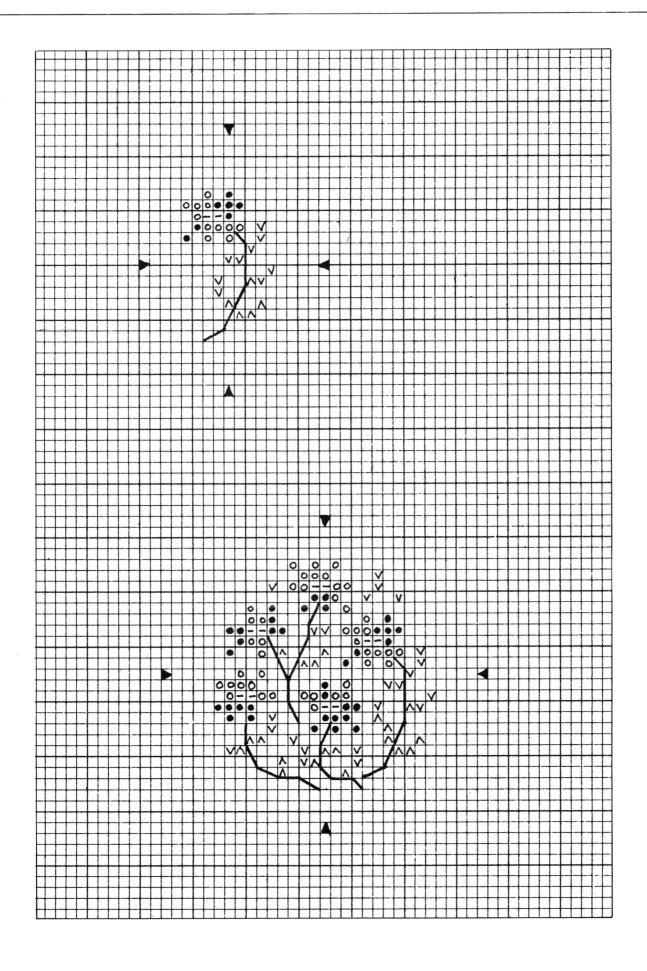

The Roses of Summer

If one flower symbolizes the beauty, warmth and brightness of summer it surely must be the rose – the queen of all flowers. In these designs, three different roses have been stitched on purchased tablelinen, creating a table setting that evokes the spirit of summer, even in winter!

THE ROSES OF SUMMER

YOU WILL NEED

For either the *Pink Rose* or *Peach Rose* tablemats, each measuring 32.5cm × 47.5cm (13in × 19in), or the *Salmon Pink Rose* napkin, measuring 37.5cm (15in) square:

Stranded embroidery cotton in the colours given in the appropriate panel
No24 tapestry needle
Sal-Em 26-count white tablelinen
(for suppliers, see page 143)

●

THE EMBROIDERY

In each case, start by determining where you are going to position your chosen design. Choose a placement that looks balanced to the eye. You may find that it is helpful to make a line of basting stitches to mark the outer perimeter of the design; you can then count inwards to a point where it is convenient to start stitching.

For each design, make the stitches over two threads of the linen, using two strands of cotton in the needle. Make sure that all top crosses face in the same direction.

When you have completed the stitching, wash the finished piece, if necessary (Sal-Em tablelinens are fully washable). Lightly press the embroidered tablemat or napkin on the wrong side.

PEACH ROSE ▼		DMC	ANCHOR	MADEIRA
●	Very light peach	948	1011	0306
X	Light peach	3779	868	0304
O	Peach	758	0403	9575
●	Dark peach	3778	1013	0303
B	Dark golden brown	611	898	2107
L	Very light grey green	524	858	1511
S	Medium khaki green	3053	844	1510
■	Dark khaki green	3051	681	1508

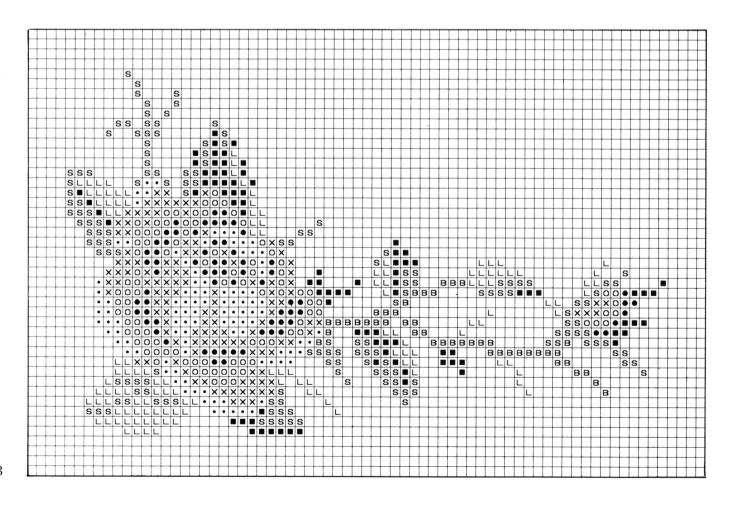

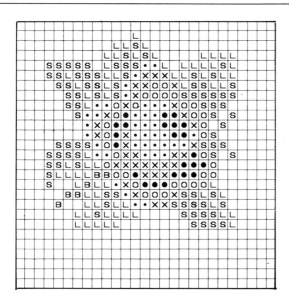

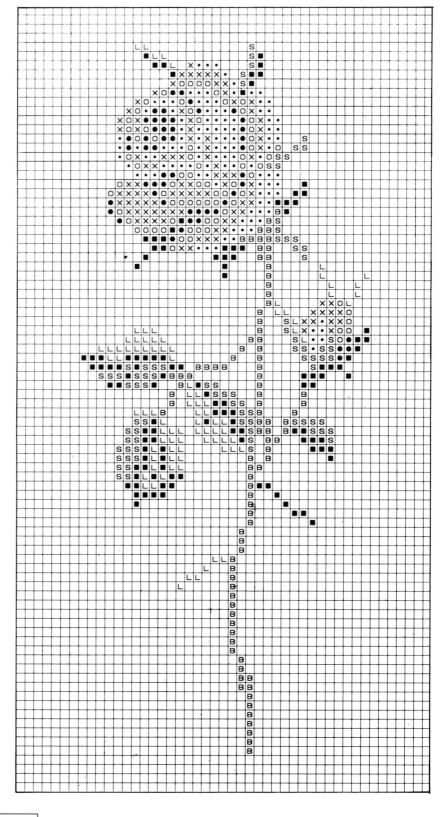

SALMON PINK ROSE ▲	DMC	ANCHOR	MADEIRA
• Shell pink	3713	48	0502
X Light salmon pink	761	8	0404
O Medium salmon pink	760	9	0405
● Dark salmon pink	3712	1023	0406
B Dark golden brown	611	898	2107
L Medium khaki green	3053	844	1510
S Clear green	3363	262	1602

PINK ROSE ▶		DMC	ANCHOR	MADEIRA
•	Very pale pink	819	271	0501
X	Shell pink	3713	48	0502
O	Light dusky pink	224	893	0813
●	Medium dusky pink	223	895	0812
B	Dark golden brown	611	898	2107
L	Very light grey green	524	858	1511
S	Light yellow green	3364	266	1501
■	Medium yellow green	3346	267	1407

The Beauty of Trees

These cool, refreshing cards featuring four trees – elm, horse chestnut, cedar and fir – are suitable for many occasions. These simple yet strong images from nature would make a perfect keepsake to treasure for their lucky recipients.

THE BEAUTY OF TREES

For the *Elm, Horse Chestnut, Cedar* or *Fir*, each set
in a card with an oval aperture measuring
12.5cm × 9cm (5in × 3½in):

*17.5cm × 12.5cm (7in × 5in) of white,
18-count Aida fabric
Stranded embroidery cotton in the colours given
in the appropriate panel
No26 tapestry needle
Card with an aperture as specified above
(for suppliers, see page 143)*

*NOTE: one skein of each colour listed is
sufficient for all four designs.*

•

THE EMBROIDERY

Prepare the fabric as described on page 8; find the
centre either by folding the fabric in half and then in
half again, and lightly pressing the folded corner, or
by marking the horizontal and vertical centre lines
with basting stitches in a light-coloured thread.
Mount the fabric in a hoop (see page 8) and start the
embroidery at the centre of the design.

Following the chart, complete all the cross
stitching, using two strands of thread in the needle.

MOUNTING AND FRAMING

Remove the finished embroidery from the frame and
remove any basting stitches. Wash if necessary, then
press lightly on the wrong side, using a steam iron.
Trim the embroidery to measure about 12mm (½in)
larger all around than the size of the card window.
Position the embroidery behind the window; open
out the self-adhesive mount; fold the card, and press
firmly to secure it. Some cards require a dab of glue
to ensure a secure and neat finish.

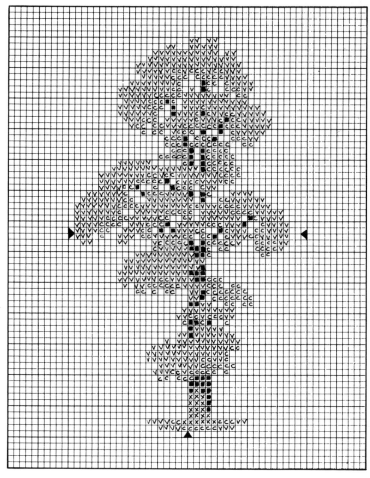

▲ Elm

TREES		ANCHOR	DMC	MADEIRA
v	Light yellow green	238	703	1307
C	Dark yellow green	258	904	1413
○	Medium green	243	988	1402
●	Dark green	245	986	1405
X	Light brown	358	433	2008
■	Dark brown	360	898	2006
•	White	1	Blanc	White

ELM ▲		ANCHOR	DMC	MADEIRA
v	Light yellow green	703	703	1307
C	Dark yellow green	258	904	1413
X	Light brown	358	433	2008
■	Dark brown	360	898	2006

HORSE CHESTNUT ▶		ANCHOR	DMC	MADEIRA
○	Medium green	243	988	1402
●	Dark green	245	986	1405
X	Light brown	358	433	2008
■	Dark brown	360	898	2006
•	White	1	Blanc	White

CEDAR ▶		ANCHOR	DMC	MADEIRA
v	Light yellow green	238	703	1307
C	Dark yellow green	258	904	1413
X	Light brown	358	433	2008
■	Dark brown	360	898	2006

FIR ▶		ANCHOR	DMC	MADEIRA
●	Dark green	245	986	1405
X	Light brown	358	433	2008
■	Dark brown	360	898	2006

► Cedar

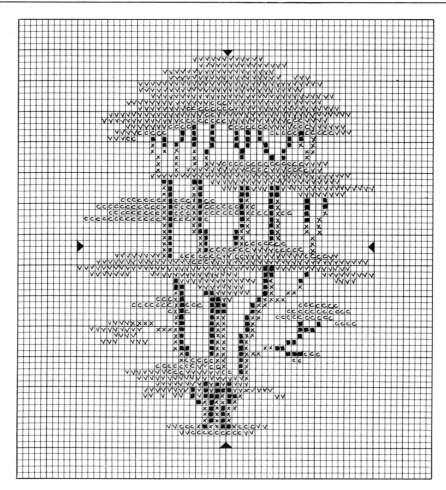

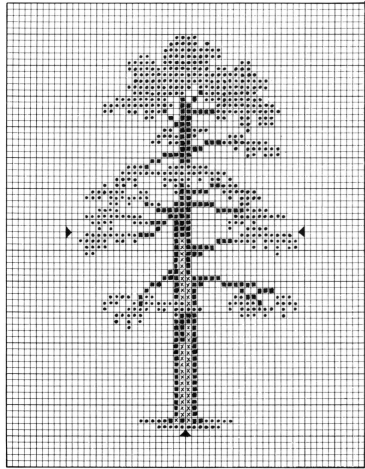

▲ Fir

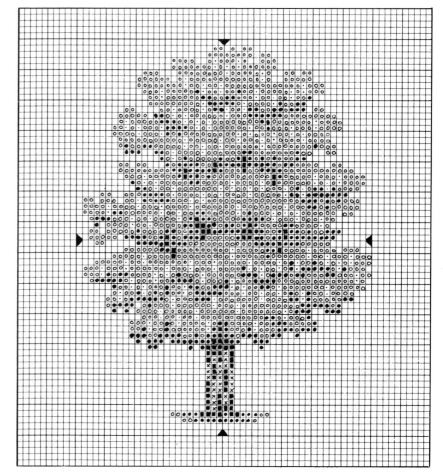

▲ Horse Chestnut

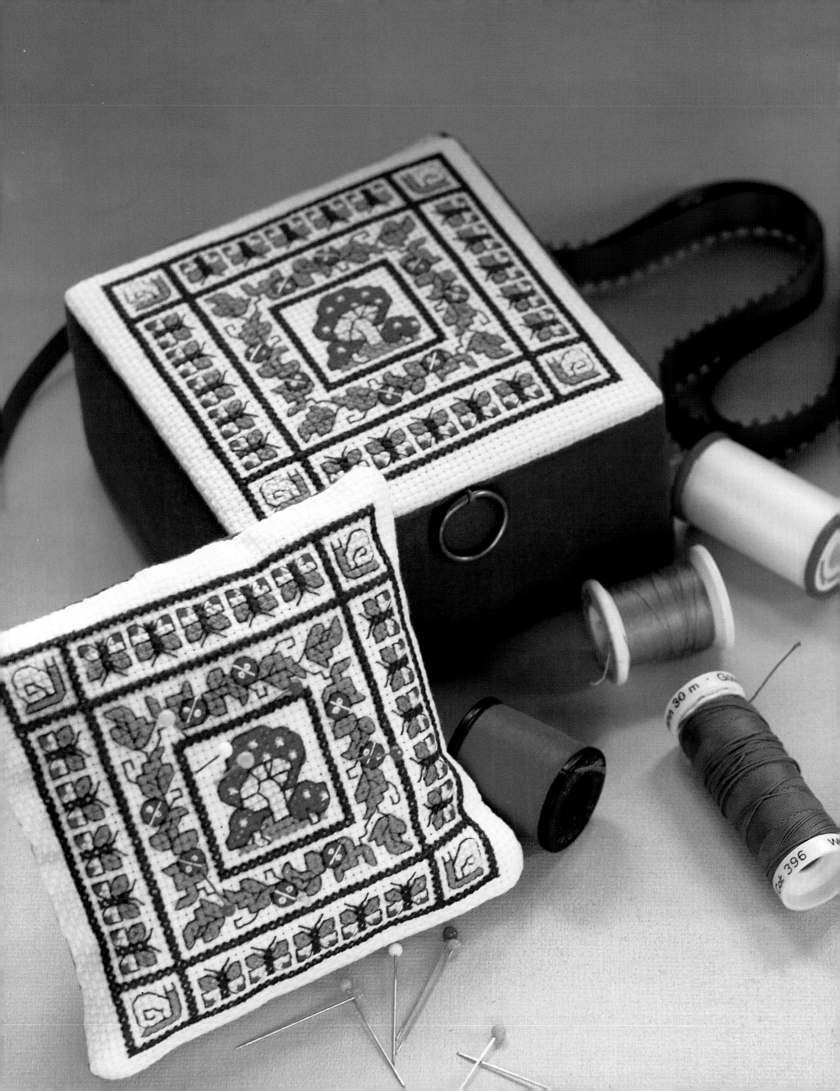

Woodland Magic

Ladybirds, butterflies, snails and toadstools create a simple square design that can be adapted to a multitude of uses. A pin cushion, needlecase and box are shown here, but the design would also make a charming birthday card, while either the outer or inner border, or both, could be used for a picture frame.

WOODLAND MAGIC

For the pin cushion, measuring
10cm (4in) square:

20cm (8in) square of white, 14-count Aida fabric
12.5cm (5in) square of green cotton fabric,
for backing
Stranded embroidery cotton in the colours
given in the panel
No26 tapestry needle
Wool, kapok or polyester filling

For the needlecase, measuring
10cm (4in) square:

30cm × 20cm (12 × 8in) of white,
14-count Aida fabric
24cm × 12.5cm (9½ × 5in) of green backing fabric
20cm × 10cm (8in × 4in) of green felt
Stranded embroidery cotton in the colours given
in the panel
No26 tapestry needle

For the box, 5cm (2in) deep, with a top measuring
10cm (4in) square:

20cm (8in) square of white, 14-count Aida fabric
Stranded embroidery cotton in the colours given
in the panel
No26 tapestry needle
Seven pieces of green cotton fabric,
each 12.5cm (5in) square
Stiff card (medium thickness) – four pieces
5cm × 10cm (2in × 4in),
and four pieces 10cm (4in) square
Lightweight polyester batting –
four pieces 5cm × 10cm (2in × 4in),
and one piece 10cm (4in) square
25cm (10in) of thin white cord
Small brass curtain ring
Glue stick
Masking tape
Strong thread for lacing

•

THE EMBROIDERY

For either the pin cushion or the box, start by preparing the fabric as described on page 8; find the centre either by folding the fabric in half and then in half again, and lightly pressing the folded corner, or by marking the horizontal and vertical centre lines with basting stitches in a light-coloured thread. Mount the fabric in a hoop (see page 8) and start the design from the centre.

If you are making the needlecase, start by folding the fabric in half and half again, to find the centre and then baste a rectangle measuring 21.5cm × 10cm (8½in × 4in) around the centre of the fabric. On the right-hand half of the rectangle (the front of the needlecase) mark the centre of this half only with horizontal and vertical lines of basting stitches in a light coloured thread. This centre is the centre of the design.

Following the chart and working from the centre outwards, complete all the cross stitching first, using two strands of thread in the needle. Finish with the backstitching, again using two strands of thread. Remove the finished embroidery from the hoop and wash if necessary, then press lightly on the wrong side, using a steam iron.

PIN CUSHION

Keeping the design centred, trim the Aida to measure 12.5cm (5in) square. Remove basting stitches. Place the embroidery and backing fabric right sides together and stitch around the sides, taking a 12mm (½in) seam allowance and leaving a small gap in one side for the filling. Trim across the seam allowance at the corners; turn the pin cushion right side out and fill tightly. Slipstitch across the opening.

NEEDLECASE

Trim the embroidery fabric, leaving a 12mm (½in) seam allowance around the basted rectangle. Remove basting stitches. Place the embroidery and backing fabric with right sides together and stitch around the edge, taking a 12mm (½in) seam allowance and leaving a small gap, for turning, on the lower edge at the blank half of the fabric. Trim across the seam allowance at the corners; turn the fabric right side out and slipstitch the gap. Using pinking shears, trim the felt to fit inside the needlecase, then attach it inside the centre fold, using small running stitches.

BOX

To prepare the side sections, first glue a piece of batting to one side of the each of the four 5cm × 10cm (2in × 4in) pieces of card. For each side, take a piece of green fabric and lay a card piece, padded side down, on the wrong side of the fabric, with an allowance of 12mm (½in) of fabric showing at each side, and a scant 15mm (⅝in) showing at the bottom edge. Fold in the sides and tape them, as shown. Bring the lower edge of the fabric up over the card; turn under a 12mm (½in) allowance along the top edge and bring it down to cover the lower raw edge of fabric. Stitch along the lower edge, so that the stitching line is just slightly to the back of the card, not along the bottom. Oversewing the edges with neat stitches, join the four sides of the box together to make a square, with the stitched lower edges facing inwards.

Take three square sections (base and inside lid) and cover one side of each with a piece of fabric: mitre the corners and fold in the sides, holding them with tape. With the fabric outside, gently push one base section into the prepared side piece and neatly oversew the bottom edge on all sides. Turn the box over and neatly stitch white cord along the top edge of one side (now the back edge), allowing the ends to run down the inside corners and onto the base. Push the second base piece, fabric side up, into the

box covering the cord ends and the back of the first base section.

Keeping the design centred, trim the embroidery to measure 12.5cm (5in) square, and remove basting stitches. Glue batting to one side of the remaining uncovered piece of card, and lace the work over the padded card (see page 10). Place the two lid sections with wrong sides together and neatly oversew the edges. Stitch the lid to the cord at the back of the box, and stitch the brass ring to the front centre edge of the lid.

WOODLAND MAGIC ▼		ANCHOR	DMC	MADEIRA
◻	Leaf green	226	702	1306
●	Brown	352	300	2304
·	Lemon	292	746	101
X	Red	47	304	511
	Dark green*	228	700	1304

Note: bks butterfly feelers, snail shells and toadstools in brown, butterfly wings, ladybirds, leaves and snail bodies in dark green* (used for bks only), and the central line down the ladybirds in lemon. Make one french knot on each side of the central line down the ladybirds, using two strands of lemon.

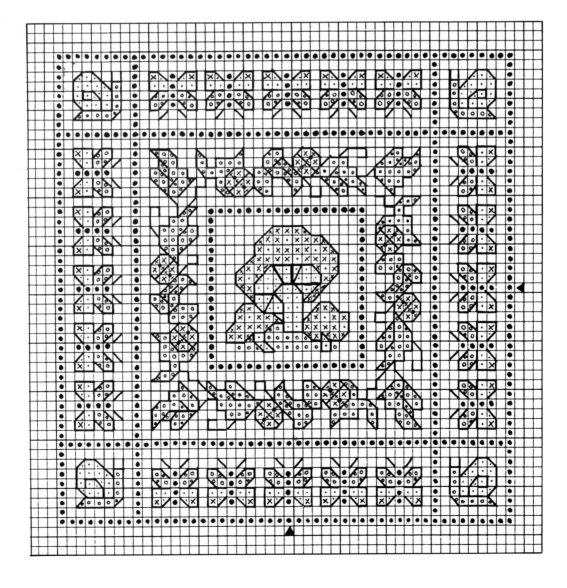

Floral Pins and Needles

Ideal gifts for a needlewoman, this needle case features a tiny cottage with a floral border while the pincushion is decorated with a matching garland of flowers.

FLORAL
PINS AND NEEDLES

YOU WILL NEED

For the Needle Case, measuring 19.5cm × 13cm (7³/₄in × 5¹/₄in) when open:

25cm × 18cm (10in × 7¹/₄in) pine green 14-count
Aida fabric
Stranded embroidery cotton in the colours
given in the panel
No24 tapestry needle
19.5cm × 13cm (7³/₄in × 5¹/₄in) printed cotton fabric,
for lining
20cm × 32cm (8in × 12³/₄in) white or cream
flannel fabric
Matching thread
80cm (32in) bias binding, 1.5cm (⁵/₈in) wide,
in a contrasting colour

For the Pincushion, measuring 11cm (4³/₄in)
in diameter:

15cm × 15cm (6in × 6in) pine green 14-count
Aida fabric

Stranded embroidery cotton in the colours
given in the panel
No24 tapestry needle
15cm × 15cm (6in × 6in) printed cotton fabric,
for backing
Matching thread
Polyester wadding (batting)

•

THE EMBROIDERY

Stretch the fabric in a hoop or frame, as explained on page 8. Following the appropriate chart, start each embroidery at the centre of the design, using two strands of embroidery cotton in the needle. Work each stitch over one block of fabric in each direction. Make sure that the top crosses of the embroidery always run in the same direction. Gently steam press the finished embroideries.

MAKING THE NEEDLE CASE

Trim the embroidery to measure 19.5cm × 13cm (7³/₄in × 5¹/₄in). Place the embroidery and lining fabric wrong sides together and baste together, close to the edges. Cut two rectangles of flannel fabric, each

PINCUSHION ▶		DMC	ANCHOR	MADEIRA
△	Pale orange	742	302	114
⊥	Soft yellow	743	305	113
▽	Pale mint	913	204	1212
◥	Pale green	3348	253	1409
◣	Soft rose	224	894	813
˥	Soft salmon	760	1023	405
■	Purple	3746	1030	804

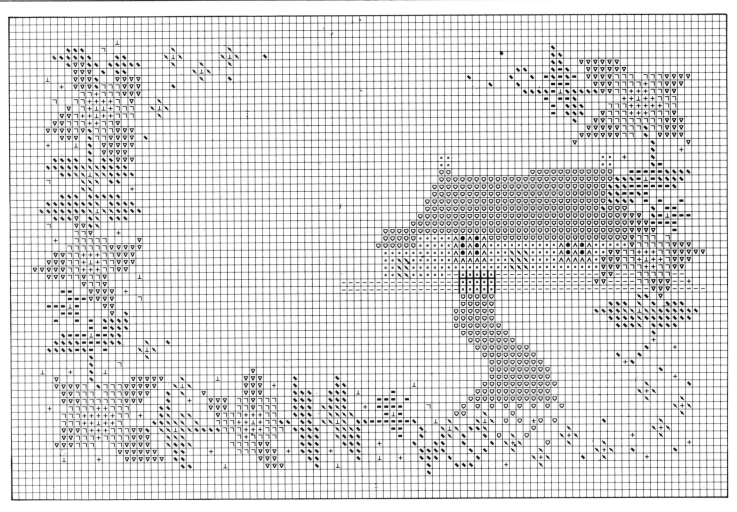

measuring 15cm × 9cm (6in × 3½in), to form 'leaves' inside the needle case. Trim the edges of the flannel pieces with pinking shears, to prevent fraying. Place these pieces centrally on the lining and stitch in place with a row of back stitches down the centre, through all thicknesses of fabric. Cut a 13cm (5¼in) length of bias binding. Fold it in half and place it across the centre to cover the stitches. Use the remaining bias binding to bind the raw edges of the needle case.

MAKING THE PINCUSHION

Trim the embroidered fabric to a circle measuring 11cm (4¾in) in diameter. Repeat with the backing fabric. Place both fabrics with right sides together and stitch all around, approximately 12mm (½in) from the edges, leaving a small gap for turning. Clip seams at intervals and turn the pincushion right side out, then stuff firmly with wadding (batting) and slip stitch the gap closed.

NEEDLE CASE ▲	DMC	ANCHOR	MADEIRA
+ Pale orange	742	302	114
⊥ Soft yellow	743	305	113
▽ Gold	743	347	0113
▽ Pale mint	913	204	1212
╲ Pale green	3348	253	1409
▭ Moss green	906	256	1411
◨ Soft rose	224	894	813
⅂ Soft salmon	760	1023	405
∘ Very pale yellow	746	275	101
∧ Very pale salmon	3779	881	2313
▬ Purple	3746	1030	804
● Black	Black	403	Black

Note: bks the cottage gate in black.

$\mathcal{R}$URAL WILDLIFE

The enchanting creatures of the woodland and country garden are celebrated in this section. The traditional sampler shown here is given a new look with this charming combination of blue tits, butterflies and berries.

HEDGEROW SAMPLER

YOU WILL NEED

For the sampler, set in a frame with an aperture measuring 28.5cm × 24.5cm (11½in × 9½in):

46cm × 38cm, (18in × 15in) of ivory,
11-count Aida fabric
Stranded embroidery cotton in the colours given
in the panel
No24 tapestry needle
Picture frame, with a cut-out as specified above
Firm card, to fit the frame
Lightweight synthetic batting, the same
size as the card
Strong thread, for mounting
Glue stick
Four small black beads and a beading needle
(optional)

●

THE EMBROIDERY

Prepare the fabric as described on page 8; find the centre either by folding the fabric in half and then in half again, and lightly pressing the folded corner, or by marking the horizontal and vertical centre lines with basting stitches in a light-coloured thread. Mount the fabric in a frame (see page 9) and start each design from the centre.

Following the chart, complete all the cross stitching first, using two strands of thread in the needle. Finish with the backstitching, again using two strands of thread. Be careful not to take dark threads across the back of the work in such a way that they show through on the right side.

The birds' eyes, indicated by black dots on the chart, can either be made with a single french knot for each, stitched with two strands of black thread, or you can use a small black bead for each eye.

MOUNTING AND FRAMING

Remove the embroidery from the frame and wash if necessary, then press lightly on the wrong side, using a steam iron and taking extra care if you have used beads for the eyes. Spread glue evenly on one side of the mounting card, and lightly press the batting to the surface. Lace the embroidery over the padded surface (see page 10). Remove basting stitches, place the embroidery in the frame, and assemble the frame according to the manufacturer's instructions.

TOP

HEDGEROW SAMPLER ▲	ANCHOR	DMC	MADEIRA
H Blue	979	312	1005
− Light yellow green	278	472	1414
+ Medium yellow green	280	733	1609
V Medium green	267	580	1608
∧ Dark green	268	935	1504

		ANCHOR	DMC	MADEIRA
•	White	1	Blanc	White
X	Brown	360	898	2006
■	Black	430	Black	Black
○	Bright red	19	817	212
●	Dark red	20	498	513

Note: bks the butterfly feelers, birds' eye lines and beaks in black, and the cherry stalks in dark green. Using two strands of thread in the needle, form each bird's eye with a french knot, unless using beads.

Wildlife Studies

Make them as five separate cards to delight your family and friends, or combine them into a single charming picture – whichever you choose, this set of wildlife studies will prove enjoyable to stitch. The individual designs are relatively simple and could prove a pleasant exercise for a child learning embroidery.

WILDLIFE STUDIES

YOU WILL NEED

For the picture, set in a frame with a centre
measuring 22.5cm × 17.5cm (9in × 7in):

*35cm × 30cm (14in × 12in) of antique white,
14-count Aida fabric
Stranded embroidery cotton in the colours given
in the panel
No26 tapestry needle
Picture frame, as specified above
Firm card, to fit the frame
Lightweight synthetic batting, the same size
as the card
Strong thread, for mounting
Glue stick*

For each card:

*15cm × 12.5cm (6in × 5in) of antique white,
14-count Aida fabric
Stranded embroidery cotton in the colours given
in the panel
No26 tapestry needle
Card with an aperture measuring 10cm × 7.5cm
(4in × 3in), designed for embroidery
(for suppliers, see page 143)*

•

THE EMBROIDERY

Prepare the fabric as described on page 8; find the
centre either by folding the fabric in half and then in
half again, and lightly pressing the folded corner, or
by marking the horizontal and vertical centre lines
with basting stitches in a light-coloured thread. If
you are making the picture, mount the fabric in a
frame (see page 9); individual designs can be
stitched without a frame.

Count out from the centre to start at an appropriate point. Following the chart, complete the
cross stitching first, using two strands of thread in
the needle. Finish with the backstitched details,
again using two strands of thread in the needle. Be
careful not to take dark threads across the back of
the work in such a way that they show through on to
the right side of the embroidery. Remove the
finished embroidery from the frame, if used, and
wash if necessary, then press lightly on the wrong
side, using a steam iron.

MOUNTING THE PICTURE

Spread glue evenly on one side of the firm card, and
lightly press the batting to the surface. Lace the
embroidery over the padded surface (see page 9),
using the basting stitches (if any) to check that the
embroidery is centred over the card. Remove
basting stitches, place the mounted embroidery
in the frame, and assemble the frame according to
the manufacturer's instructions.

THE CARDS

For each card, trim the embroidery to measure about
12mm (½in) larger all around than the size of the
card window. Remove basting stitches. Position the
embroidery behind the window; open out the self-
adhesive mount; fold the card, and press firmly to
secure it. Some cards require a dab of glue to ensure
a secure and neat finish.

WILDLIFE STUDIES ▶	ANCHOR	DMC	MADEIRA
• White	1	Blanc	White
– Silver grey	397	453	1807
I Medium grey	399	318	1802
X Dark grey	400	317	1714
■ Black	403	310	Black
C Light warm brown	369	435	2010
O Medium warm brown	370	433	2008
+ Dark warm brown	371	739	2303
● Dark brown	905	3781	2106
V Light grass green	226	702	1306
∧ Medium grass green	228	700	1304

*Note: bks ears of squirrel, badger, rabbit and pole cat in black,
and badger's eye in white.*

Spring Creatures

These delightful designs feature a goose and lamb, both surrounded by spring flowers; they have been made up as gift items in small porcelain and glass boxes, but would also make wonderful Easter cards or small pictures for childrens' rooms.

SPRING CREATURES

For the *Goose with violets*, set in a frosted glass bowl, 7.5cm (3in) in diameter:

*15cm (6in) square of white, 18-count Aida fabric
Stranded embroidery cotton in the colours given
in the panel
No26 tapestry needle
Frosted glass bowl (for suppliers, see page 143)*

For the *Lamb with blossoms*, set in an oval porcelain box, 8cm (3¼in) long:

*15cm (6in) square of pale pink, 18-count Aida fabric
Stranded embroidery cotton in the colours given
in the panel
No26 tapestry needle
Pale pink oval porcelain box
(for suppliers, see page 143)*

NOTE: If you are stitching both designs, you will only require one skein of each of the colours listed.

•

THE EMBROIDERY

For each design, prepare the fabric, marking the centre of the design with horizontal and vertical lines of basting stitches in a light-coloured thread. You can either set the fabric in a hoop or, for these small-scale designs, hold the work in the hand as you embroider. Start the embroidery from the centre and work outwards, working the cross stitches first and then finishing with the backstitching. Use one strand of embroidery cotton in the needle for both cross stitches and backstitching.

Wash the finished embroidery, if necessary, and lightly press with a steam iron. It is a good idea to leave the basting stitches in at this stage, as they will prove useful in helping you to centre your design in the lid.

ASSEMBLING THE LID

Place the finished embroidery face up on a firm, flat surface. Gently remove all parts from the lid of the trinket box. Use the rim of the lid and the basting stitches to centre the design. Using a hard pencil, draw a line on the fabric, around the outer edge of the lid, then cut along the drawn line, trimming the fabric to shape. Remove the basting stitches.

To assemble the lid, replace the clear acetate and place your design in the lid, with the right side to the acetate. Place the sponge behind your design. Push the metal locking disc very firmly into place, using thumb pressure, with the raised side of the disc facing the sponge. When the locking disc is tightly in position, use a little glue to secure the flock lining card to it.

GOOSE WITH VIOLETS ▶			DMC	ANCHOR	MADEIRA
Cross	Half Cross				
M		Mauve	554	96	0711
•		White	White	2	White
/		Very light grey	762	397	1804
X	\	Very light grey green	524	858	1511
P		Medium salmon pink	761	8	0404
O		Light pink	3713	48	0502
L		Light orange	402	1047	2307
Y		Light yellow	745	300	0111
		Medium grey green*	522	860	1513
		Medium orange*	722	323	0307
		Dark grey*	414	235	1801

Note: backstitch the stems on the wreath in medium grey green, the feet of the goose in medium orange* and the goose outline in dark grey* (starred colours are used for backstitch only).*

LAMB WITH BLOSSOMS ▶			DMC	ANCHOR	MADEIRA
Cross	Half Cross				
•		White	White	2	White
/		Very light grey	762	397	1804
X		Medium grey	318	399	1802
	I	Medium grey green	522	860	1513
P		Medium salmon pink	761	8	0404
Y		Light yellow	745	300	0111
S		Very light grey green	524	858	1511
		Dark grey*	414	235	1801

Note: backstitch the lamb outline in dark grey (used for backstitch only), and the flower stems in medium grey green.*

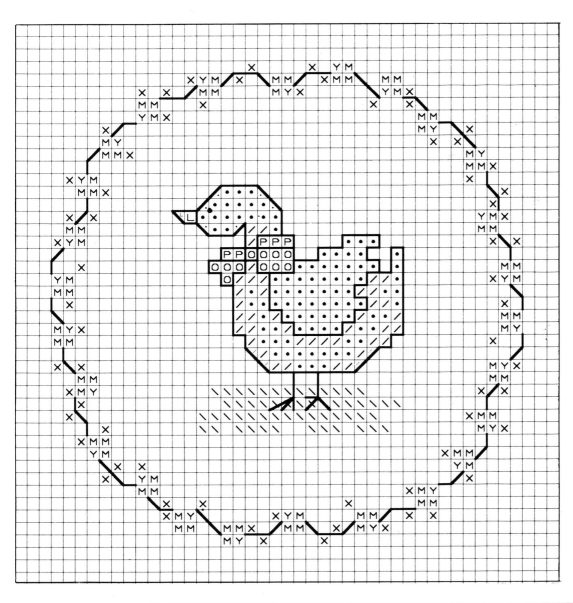

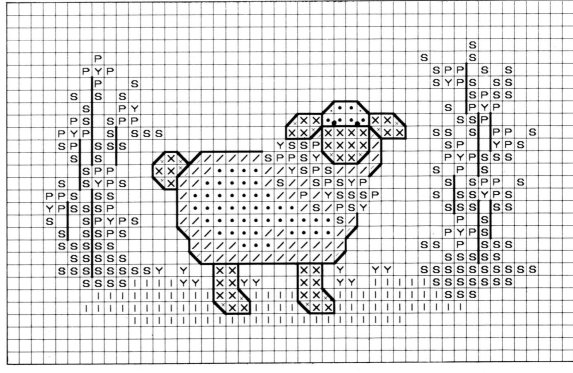

Butterflies

The ecological way to mount and frame butterflies is demonstrated in these two charming pictures, each displaying a pair of beautifully observed butterflies. Stitch and frame them as shown here or, alternatively, you might embroider all four on a single piece of fabric and frame them in a traditional glass case.

BUTTERFLIES

YOU WILL NEED

For either the *Gatekeeper and Tortoiseshell* or the
Painted lady and Peacock picture,
each set in a frame with a centre measuring
14cm × 9.5cm (5½ × 3½in):

*25cm × 20cm (10in × 8in) of antique white,
14-count Aida fabric
Stranded embroidery cotton in the colours given
in the appropriate panel*

*No24 tapestry needle
Picture frame, with an aperture as specified above
Firm card, to fit the frame
Lightweight synthetic batting, the same size
as the card
Strong thread, for mounting
Glue stick*

*NOTE: if you only wish to stitch one
of these pictures, you
will not require every colour
listed – check with the relevant chart;
one skein of each colour listed is
sufficient for both pictures.*

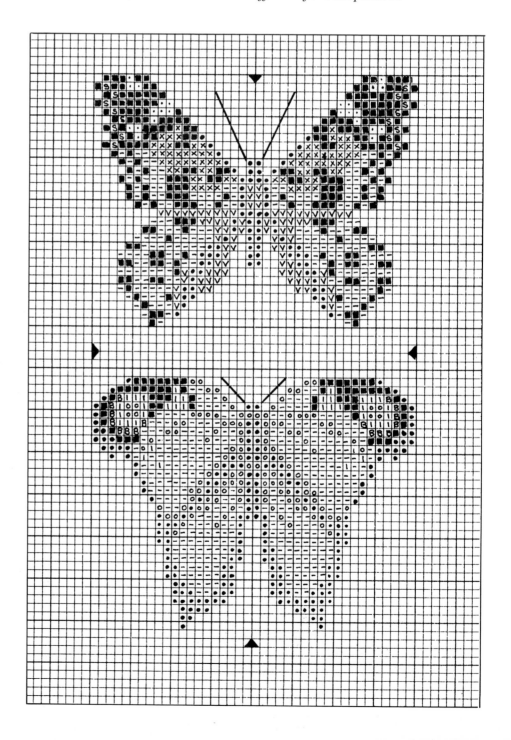

Top: Painted Lady
Bottom: Peacock

Top: Gatekeeper
Bottom: Tortoiseshell

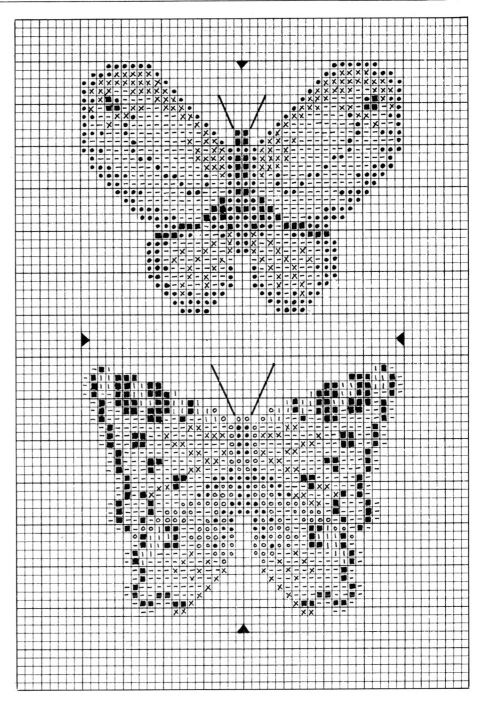

THE EMBROIDERY

Prepare the fabric as described on page 8; find the centre either by folding the fabric in half and then in half again, and lightly pressing the folded corner, or by marking the horizontal and vertical centre lines with basting stitches in a light-coloured thread. Mount the fabric in a frame (see page 9) and count out from the centre to start the design at an appropriate point.

Following the chart, complete all the cross stitching first, using two strands of thread in the needle. Finish with the antennae, again using two strands of thread. Be careful not to take dark threads across the back of the work in such a way that they show through on the right side.

MOUNTING AND FRAMING

Remove the finished embroidery from the frame and wash if necessary, then press lightly on the wrong side, using a steam iron. Spread glue evenly on one side of the mounting card, and lightly press the batting to the surface. Lace the embroidery over the padded surface (see page 10), using the basting stitches (if any) to check that the embroidery is centred over the card. Remove basting stitches, place the mounted embroidery in the frame, and assemble the frame according to the manufacturer's instructions.

BUTTERFLIES ▲		ANCHOR	DMC	MADEIRA
■	Black	403	310	Black
●	Dark brown	905	3031	2003
O	Rust	370	433	2008
v	Light brown	375	420	2104
-	Light orange	314	741	201
X	Deep orange	316	740	203
I	Lemon yellow	293	727	110
B	Pale blue	128	775	1101
•	White	1	Blanc	White
S	Grey	399	318	1802

Note: embroider antennae in dark brown, using two strands of thread in the needle and making each antenna with one long straight stitch.

Village Ducks Bath Set

Ducklings waddle behind their
mother along a towel border and
across the flap of a make-up purse.
This charming design would also
make a pretty greetings card
for any occasion.

VILLAGE DUCKS
BATH SET

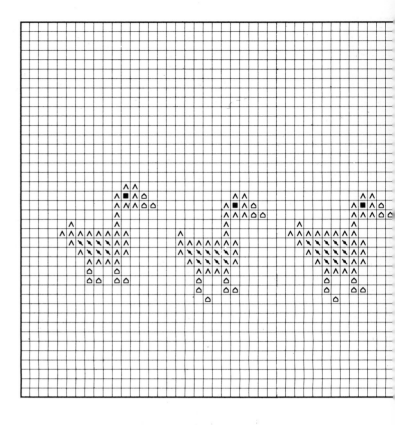

YOU WILL NEED

For the Towel Border:

*52cm (20³⁄₄in) length of 5cm (2in) white Aida band
with yellow edging
Stranded embroidery cotton in the colours given in
the panel
No24 tapestry needle
Hand towel
Matching thread*

*For the Make-Up Purse, measuring 17cm × 13.5cm
(6³⁄₄in × 5³⁄₈in) when closed:*

*45cm × 25cm (18in × 10in) blue 14-count
Aida fabric
Stranded embroidery cotton in the colours given
in the panel
No24 tapestry needle
38cm × 17cm (15¹⁄₄in × 6³⁄₄in) cotton lining fabric
85cm (34in) yellow cotton bias binding,
1.5cm (⁵⁄₈in) wide
Matching thread*

•

THE EMBROIDERY

Stretch the fabric in a hoop or frame, as explained
on page 8. Following the appropriate chart, work
each embroidery using two strands of embroidery
cotton in the needle. Work each stitch over one
block of fabric in each direction. Make sure the top
crosses run in the same direction.

For the make-up purse, position the design at
one end of the fabric and stitch your chosen initials
in the area indicated. Gently steam press the
finished embroideries on the wrong side.

MAKING THE TOWEL BORDER

Fold in 12mm (¹⁄₂in) at each end of the Aida band.
Pin the strip in place across the width of the towel
(covering the area that has no pile). With matching
sewing thread, hand-stitch the band in place.

MAKING THE MAKE-UP PURSE

Place the lining fabric, right side up, centrally over
the back of the embroidery. Baste the two together

close to the edge of the lining fabric. Trim the Aida
to match the size of the lining. Cut a 17cm (6³⁄₄in)
length of bias binding and use it to bind the short
end, furthest away from the embroidered area.
Handstitch in place. Fold up this end to form a
pocket. The embroidered part will form the flap of
the purse; cut the corners to a neat, rounded shape.
Now use the rest of the bias binding to bind the
remaining raw edges.

TOWEL BORDER ▲		DMC	ANCHOR	MADEIRA
⊙	White	White	1	White
■	Black	310	403	Black
⊟	Dark grey	317	400	1714
⊡	Mid grey	415	399	1803
⊥	Pale grey	762	234	1804
∧	Pale yellow	727	289	103
◣	Yellow	444	297	105
△	Orange	742	313	2307

MAKE-UP PURSE ▶		DMC	ANCHOR	MADEIRA
⊙	White	White	1	White
■	Black	310	403	Black
⊟	Dark grey	317	400	1714
⊡	Mid grey	415	399	1803
⊥	Pale grey	762	234	1804
∧	Pale steel	3752	1038	1105
△	Tan brown	782	901	2210
◣	Pale yellow	727	289	103
+	Yellow	444	297	105
◇	Orange	742	313	2307
⋈	Steel blue	931	779	1712

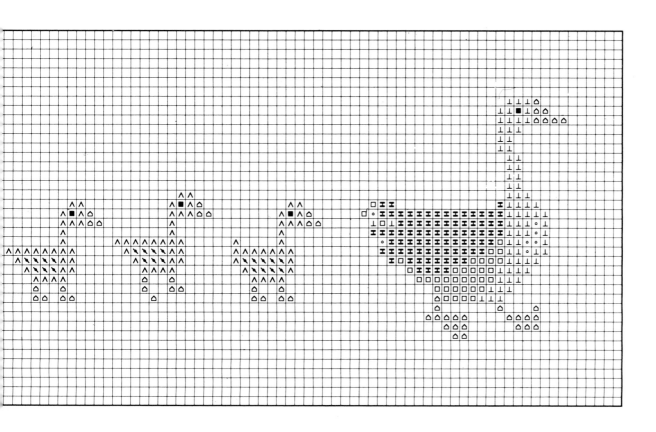

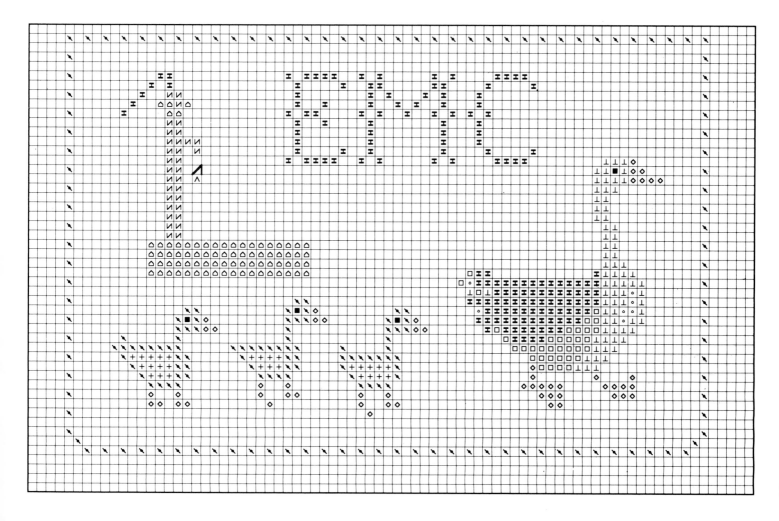

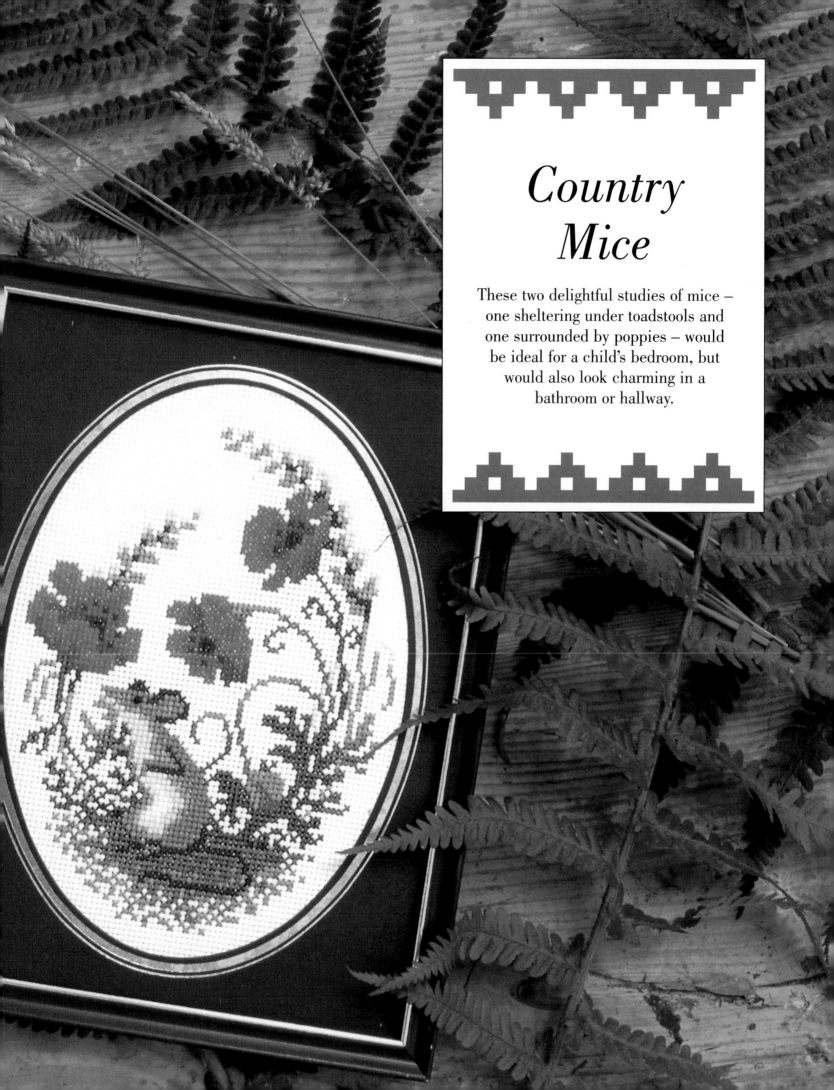

Country Mice

These two delightful studies of mice –
one sheltering under toadstools and
one surrounded by poppies – would
be ideal for a child's bedroom, but
would also look charming in a
bathroom or hallway.

COUNTRY MICE

YOU WILL NEED

For either the *Toadstool Mouse* or the *Poppy Mouse* picture, each set in a frame measuring 23cm × 18cm (9in × 7in), with an oval cut-out measuring 19cm × 14cm (7½ × 5½in):

30cm × 27.5cm (12in × 11in) of white, 14-count Aida fabric
Stranded embroidery cotton in the colours given in the panel

No24 tapestry needle
One small dark brown or black bead (optional)
Picture frame
Picture mount to fit the frame, with an oval aperture as specified above
Firm card, to fit the frame
Lightweight synthetic batting, the same size as the card
Strong thread, for mounting
Glue stick

NOTE: one skein of each colour listed is sufficient for both pictures.

Poppy Mouse ▶

THE EMBROIDERY

Prepare the fabric as described on page 8; find the centre either by folding the fabric in half and then in half again, and lightly pressing the folded corner, or by marking the horizontal and vertical centre lines with basting stitches in a light-coloured thread. Mount the fabric in a frame (see page 9) and count out from the centre to start the design at an appropriate point.

Following the chart, complete all the cross stitching first, using two strands of thread in the needle. Finish with the eye of the mouse, which is formed by one dark brown cross stitch. If you choose, you may add a small bead to the eye, which will bring it to life.

MOUNTING AND FRAMING

Remove the finished embroidery from the frame and wash if necessary, then press lightly on the wrong side, using a steam iron. Spread glue evenly on one side of the firm card, and lightly press the batting to the surface. Lace the embroidery over the padded surface (see page 10), using the basting stitches (if any) to check that the embroidery is centred over the card. Remove basting stitches, place the mounted embroidery in the frame, behind the oval mount, and assemble the frame according to the manufacturer's instructions.

COUNTRY MICE		ANCHOR	DMC	MADEIRA
•	White	2	Blanc	White
−	Cream	300	745	111
C	Light green	238	703	1307
○	Medium green	258	904	1413
●	Dark green	245	986	1405
2	Bright red	335	606	209
3	Medium red	19	817	212
4	Dark red	20	498	513
I	Beige	381	938	2005
H	Light brown	374	420	2104
■	Dark brown	380	839	1913

COUNTRY COTTAGES

*On the following pages,
idyllic country cottages are
captured in cross stitch,
starting with this small
cushion. This design is
reminiscent of traditional
sampler styles, with its rows
of stylized flowers and leaves,
but it has been interpreted
in the style of the typical
English cottage garden.*

'IN A COTTAGE GARDEN'

YOU WILL NEED

For the pillow, measuring 23cm (9in) square,
excluding the lace trim:

30cm (12in) square of white, 18-count Aida fabric
Stranded embroidery cotton in the colours given in
the panel
No26 tapestry needle
1.1m (1⅓yds) of gathered broderie anglaise,
3cm (1¼in) wide
25cm (10in) square of backing fabric
4 white ribbon roses
Polyester filling
Pot pourri (optional)

●

THE EMBROIDERY

Prepare the fabric as described on page 8; find the
centre by folding, and mark the horizontal and
vertical centre lines with basting stitches in a light-
coloured thread. Set the fabric in a frame or hoop
(see pages 8-9), and count out from the centre to
start stitching at a point convenient to you.

One thread of cotton was used in the needle for
cross stitches and for backstitch throughout the
design. Work all cross stitches first, making sure
that all top stitches run in the same direction.
Finally, work all backstitch details.

MAKING THE PILLOW

Gently handwash the finished piece, if necessary,
and lightly press with a steam iron on the wrong
side. Trim the embroidered fabric to measure 25cm
(10in) square. Pin the broderie anglaise to the right
side of the embroidery, with the decorative edge
facing inwards. Trim the ends, if necessary, and
join them with a neat french seam.

Gathering it slightly at the corners, baste the
broderie anglaise in place, lying just inside the
12mm (½in) seam allowance. With right sides
together, pin and stitch the backing fabric and
embroidered piece together, leaving a gap of 5cm
(2in) at one side.

Clip the corners; turn the cover right side out,
and fill with polyester, adding the pot pourri if this
is to be included. Slipstitch the opening, and finish
by stitching a ribbon rose in each corner of the
cushion.

IN A COTTAGE GARDEN ▶		DMC	ANCHOR	MADEIRA
⬙	Medium grey green	522	860	1513
⬡	Light grey green	523	859	1512
·	Very light grey green	524	858	1511
▲	Medium golden brown	611	898	2107
⊟	Golden brown	612	832	2108
◪	Medium antique violet	3041	870	0806
▣	Light antique violet	3042	869	0807
▯	Pale cream	822	390	1908
⋀	Medium beige grey	642	853	1906
⟍	Light beige grey	644	830	1907
◪	Sky blue	3752	976	1001
◎	Silver grey	415	398	1803
Y	Yellow	744	301	0112
V	Apple green	368	261	1310
●	Clear green	3363	262	1311
⊞	Light clear green	3364	266	1501
Z	Medium salmon pink	760	9	0405
X	Light salmon pink	761	8	0404
╱	Light shell pink	3713	48	0502
■	Dark grey	3022	392	1903
	White*	White	2	White

Note: bks house walls, door, roof and outer windows in dark grey;
use clear green for inner and outer border, and white (used for*
bks only) for window panes.

119

Traditional Cottages

The English cottage is known all over the world as exemplifying the cottage at its most charming and traditional. In these designs, three different cottages have been stitched to create a set of delightful small pictures.

TRADITIONAL COTTAGES

YOU WILL NEED

For each Traditional Cottage picture, set in a rectangular frame, measuring 15cm × 12.5cm (6in × 5in):

22.5cm × 20cm (9in × 8in) of antique white, 18-count Aida fabric
Stranded embroidery cotton in the colours given in the appropriate panel
No 26 tapestry needle
Wooden frame, as specified above
Strong thread and cardboard, for mounting

NOTE: these designs have been stitched as miniatures; should you prefer larger pictures, simply use linen with a coarser weave, and two strands of embroidery cotton. Several shades of cotton have been used in all three pictures. If you are making the set, you will only require one skein of each colour.

•

THE EMBROIDERY

Prepare the fabric as described on page 8; find the centre by folding, and mark the horizontal and vertical centre lines with basting stitches in a light-coloured thread. Set the fabric in a hoop or frame, and count out from the centre to start stitching at a point convenient to you.

One thread of cotton was used in the needle for cross stitches and one for backstitch throughout these designs. Work all cross stitches first, making sure that all top stitches run in the same direction. Finally, work all backstitch details. When stitching The Lodge, the effect of diamond window panes is made by taking long diagonal stitches across each window pane, using one strand of cotton. Use the photograph as a guide when making these stitches.

FINISHING

Gently handwash the finished piece, if necessary, and lightly press with a steam iron on the wrong side. Stretch and mount the embroidery as explained on page 10. Insert it into the frame. Simple wooden frames were used with each of these pictures to avoid overwhelming the design.

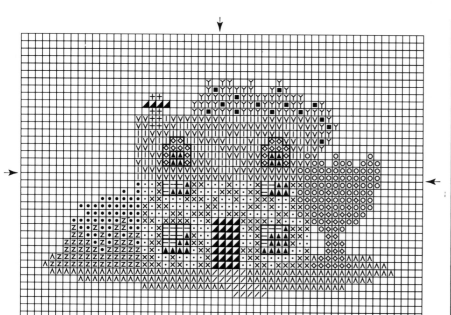

BROADWAY COTTAGE ◄			DMC	ANCHOR	MADEIRA
Cross	Half Cross				
◤		Red brown	433	371	2303
▲	▶	Dark steel grey	414	235	1801
−		Medium steel grey	318	399	1802
✕		Medium straw	3046	887	2206
·		Light straw	3047	886	2205
▪		Light salmon pink	761	8	0404
⊙	∧	Light olive green	3053	860	1605
●		Clear green	3363	262	1311
Z		Light grey green	523	859	1509
Y		Very light grey green	524	858	1511
◇		Medium golden brown	611	898	2107
+		Dark golden brown	610	905	1914
V		Medium grey brown	642	392	1906
I		Light grey brown	644	830	1907
	⟋	Tan	437	362	2012
		White*	White	2	White
		Very dark grey*	844	401	1810

Note: bks window panes with white and dormers, window frames and door with very dark grey* (both used for bks only).*

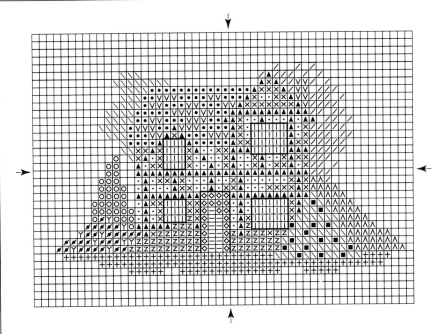

THE LODGE ►			DMC	ANCHOR	MADEIRA
Cross	Half Cross				
▲		Medium golden brown	611	898	2107
Z		Clear green	3363	262	1311
∧		Khaki	3013	854	1605
⊙		Red brown	433	371	2303
V		Medium golden tan	420	889	2010
·		Ecru	Ecru	926	2101
✕		Pale beige	3033	392	1903
◇		Medium grey brown	642	399	1906
−		Light grey brown	644	830	1907
■		Light sallmon pink	761	8	0404
Y		Yellow	744	301	0112
I		Dark steel grey	414	400	1801
⌀		Apple green	368	261	1310
⟍		Light grey green	523	859	1509
○	⟋	Light olive green	3053	860	1605
	⊞	Tan	437	362	2012
		Dark grey*	844	401	1810
		White*	White	2	White

Note: bks window frames and door in very dark grey*, and window panes in white* (both used for bks only).

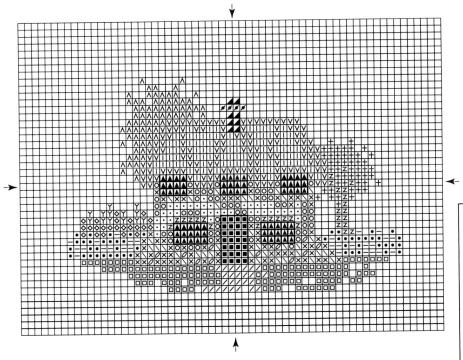

BADGER'S COTTAGE ◄			DMC	ANCHOR	MADEIRA
Cross	Half Cross				
◢		Dark golden brown	610	905	1914
⌀		Medium golden tan	420	889	2010
V		Medium straw	3046	887	2206
I		Light straw	3047	886	2205
▲		Dark grey	645	400	1811
·		White	White	2	White
○		Light silver grey	762	397	1804
■		Medium pink brown	3064	378	2310
Z		Medium golden brown	611	898	2107
✕		Light olive green	3053	860	1605
⌀		Light salmon pink	760	9	0405
⟍		Very light grey green	524	858	1511
	⟋	Tan	437	368	2012
⊙		Medium grey brown	642	392	1906
−		Light grey brown	644	830	1907
	∧	Light grey green	523	859	1512
⊞	⊡	Clear green	3363	262	1311
◇		Apple green	368	261	1310
Y		Light blue	3752	976	1710
		Very dark grey*	844	401	1810

Note: bks window frames and door in very dark grey* (used for bks only), and window panes in white.

Spring Cottage

A half-timbered cottage stands under a canopy of blossom in a spring landscape that echoes the freshness of the season. This is the first of four seasonal pictures, and will bring a touch of spring to any home.

SPRING COTTAGE

YOU WILL NEED

For the Spring Cottage picture, set in a mount with a cut-out measuring 16.5cm × 21.5cm (6½in × 8½in):

30cm × 35cm (12in × 14in) of antique white, 14-count Aida fabric
Stranded embroidery cotton in the colours given in the panel
No 26 tapestry needle
Wooden frame, measuring 26cm × 30cm (10⅜in × 12in)
Rectangular mount, cut to fit the frame, with cut-out as specified above
Strong thread and cardboard, for mounting

●

THE EMBROIDERY

Prepare the fabric as described on page 8; find the centre by folding, and mark the horizontal and vertical centre lines with basting stitches in a light-coloured thread. Set the fabric in a frame or hoop and count out from the centre to start stitching at a point convenient to you.

Two threads of cotton were used in the needle for cross stitches and one for backstitch, *unless* otherwise stated on the colour key. Work all full cross stitches first, and then the half crosses, taking them over one block of fabric. Make sure that all top stitches run in the same direction. Finally, work all backstitch details.

FINISHING

Gently handwash the finished piece, if necessary, and lightly press with a steam iron on the wrong side. Finally, stretch and mount the embroidery as explained on page 10. Insert it into the frame, behind the rectangular mount. A subtle wooden frame has been used for all four seasonal cottage pictures, and the colour of the mount has been especially selected in each case to echo colours predominant in the design.

SPRING COTTAGE ▶			DMC	ANCHOR	MADEIRA
Cross	Half Cross				
⊞		White	White	2	White
⊙		Medium olive green	3053	859	1510
▲		Dark beige grey	640	903	1905
▽		Medium beige grey	642	392	1906
⫾		Light beige grey	644	830	1907
◉		Dark olive green	3052	844	1509
◢		Dark brown	839	360	1914
⊘		Medium salmon pink	760	9	0405
∧		Light salmon pink	761	8	0404
■		Dark grey	844	401	1810
T		Golden tan	420	375	2104
●		Light blue grey	927	849	1708
◪	╱	Medium grey green	522	859	1513
⊡	▫	Very light grey green	524	858	1511
L		Light yellow	744	301	0112
Y		Very light yellow	745	300	0111
	◥	Light tan	437	362	2012
	⊏	Very light tan	738	942	2013
◈		Apple green	368	261	1310
⊙		Clear green	3363	262	1311
⊔		Light clear green	3364	843	1603
⊟		Beige	3033	387	2001
	N	Very soft blue	3753	158	1014
⊠		Golden brown	612	832	2108
		Dark golden brown*	611	898	2107

Note: bks roof, house, door and birds with one strand only of dark golden brown (used for bks only) in the needle, and window panes with two strands of white; when using very soft blue, stitch with one strand only; very light green is used for cross stitches in the background and half cross stitches in the foreground; very light tan, apple green, and very soft blue are used for half cross stitches only.*

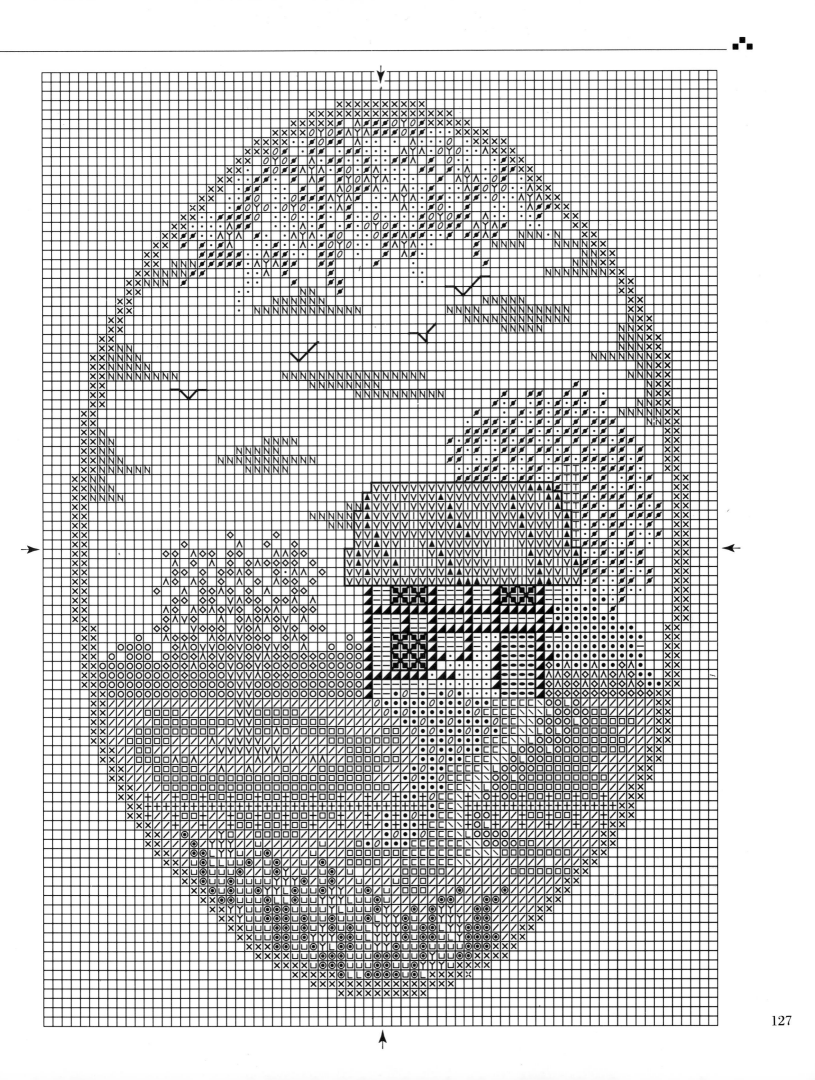

Summer Cottage

This picture offers what has to be the quintessential image of an English summer scene – the golden thatched cottage covered with creepers and climbing roses and surrounded by the typical English cottage garden, a riot of scent and colour.

SUMMER COTTAGE

YOU WILL NEED

For the Summer Cottage picture, set in a mount with a cut-out measuring 16.5cm × 21.5cm (6½in × 8½in):

30cm × 35cm (12in × 14in) of antique white, 14-count Aida fabric
Stranded embroidery cotton in the colours given in the panel
No 26 tapestry needle
Wooden frame, measuring 26cm × 30cm (10⅜in × 12in)
Rectangular mount, cut to fit the frame, with cut-out as specified above
Strong thread and cardboard, for mounting

•

THE EMBROIDERY

Prepare the fabric as described on page 8; find the centre by folding, and mark the horizontal and vertical centre lines with basting stitches in a light-coloured thread. Set the fabric in a frame or hoop, and count out from the centre to start stitching at a point convenient to you.

Two threads of cotton were used in the needle for cross stitches and one for backstitch, *unless* otherwise stated on the colour key. Work all full cross stitches first, and then the half crosses, taking them over one block of fabric. Make sure that all top stitches run in the same direction. Finally, work all backstitch details.

FINISHING

Gently handwash the finished piece, if necessary, and lightly press with a steam iron on the wrong side. Stretch and mount the embroidery as explained on page 10. Insert it into the frame, behind the rectangular mount. A subtle wooden frame has been used for all four seasonal cottage pictures, and the colour of the mount has been especially selected in each case to echo colours predominant in the design.

SUMMER COTTAGE ▶			DMC	ANCHOR	MADEIRA
Cross	Half Cross				
⊠		Golden brown	612	832	2108
◤		Dark golden brown	611	898	2107
⊙		Soft apple green	368	261	1310
●		Clear green	3363	262	1311
⌐	◿	Medium grey green	522	859	1513
◪		Medium straw	3047	887	2206
⌶		Light straw	3046	886	2205
▪		Very dark grey	844	401	1810
Y		Yellow	744	301	0112
+		Soft antique mauve	3042	869	0807
▲		Medium salmon pink	760	9	0405
◓		Light salmon pink	761	8	0404
–		Soft shell pink	3713	48	0502
⊏		Soft clear green	3364	266	1501
∧		Very light grey green	524	858	1511
⁄		White	White	2	White
⊘		Pale cream	822	390	1908
Z		Medium olive green	3053	844	1510
◉		Medium grey blue	926	779	1707
T		Light grey blue	927	849	1708
⊔		Very light grey blue	928	900	1709
	⊡	Light beige grey	644	830	1907
	⋁	Medium beige grey	642	392	1906
	◈	Pale blue	3752	9159	1002

Note: bks roof, house, door and window surrounds with one strand only of medium golden brown in the needle, and window panes with two strands of white; use one strand only when making half cross stitches with pale blue.

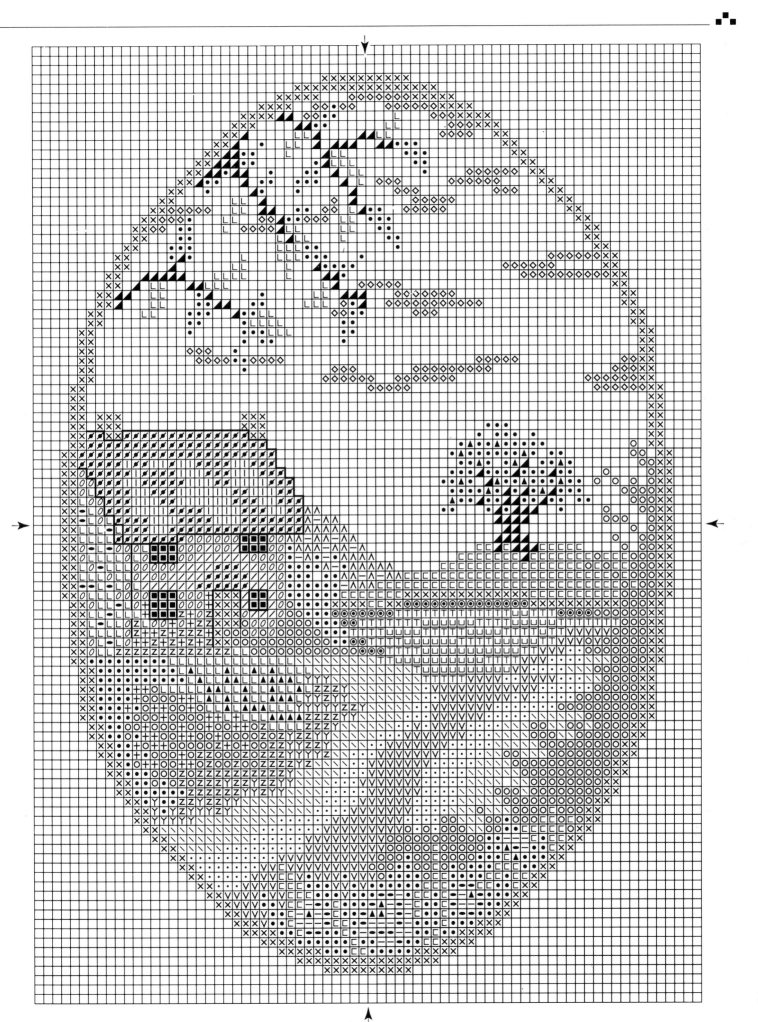

Autumn Cottage

'Season of mists and mellow fruitfulness' – the autumn of John Keats is also a time of ripening and harvest, golden fruit and falling leaves and, everywhere, rich autumnal colours. Here a brick cottage nestles behind an old grey stone wall, close to the splendour of a tree in all its autumn foliage.

AUTUMN COTTAGE

YOU WILL NEED

For the Autumn Cottage picture, set in a mount with a cut-out measuring 16.5cm × 21.5cm (6½in × 8½in):

30cm × 35cm (12in × 14in) of antique white, 14-count Aida fabric
Stranded embroidery cotton in the colours given in the panel
No26 tapestry needle
Wooden frame, measuring 26cm × 30cm (10⅜in × 12in)
Rectangular mount, cut to fit the frame, with a cut-out as specified above
Strong thread and cardboard, for mounting

●

THE EMBROIDERY

Prepare the fabric as described on page 8; find the centre by folding, and mark the horizontal and vertical centre lines with basting stitches in a light-coloured thread. Set the fabric in a frame or hoop and count out from the centre to start stitching at a point convenient to you.

Two threads of cotton were used in the needle for cross stitches and one for backstitch *unless* otherwise stated on the colour key. Work all full cross stitches first, and then the half crosses, taking them over one block of fabric. Make sure that all top stitches run in the same direction. Finally, work all backstitch details.

FINISHING

Gently handwash the finished piece, if necessary, and lightly press with a steam iron on the wrong side. Finally, stretch and mount the embroidery as explained on page 10. Insert it into the frame, behind the rectangular mount. A subtle wooden frame has been used for all seasonal cottage pictures, and the colour of the mount has been especially selected in each case to echo colours predominant in the design.

AUTUMN COTTAGE ▶			DMC	ANCHOR	MADEIRA
Cross	**Half Cross**				
☒		Golden brown	612	832	2108
▲		Medium steel grey	647	8581	1813
I		Light steel grey	648	900	1814
O		Clear green	3363	262	1311
◪		Medium golden brown	611	898	2107
●		Dark peach	351	10	0214
◈		Medium peach	352	9	0303
Y		Yellow	744	301	0112
■		Very dark grey	844	401	1810
V	◺	Light golden brown	613	831	2109
T		Light tan	437	362	2012
─		Very light tan	738	942	2013
◩	⁄	Dusky peach	3773	883	2312
⊏		Soft peach	754	6	0305
	⦁	Soft clear green	3364	843	1603
	N	Very light grey blue	928	900	1709
Z		Tan †	420	375	2104
		Dark straw †	3045	888	2103
		†Combine one strand of each			
		White*	White	2	White

Note: bks roof, leaves, door and apples with one strand only of medium golden brown in the needle, and window panes with two strands of white* (used for bks only).

Winter Cottage

This is a classic winter scene – the Cotswold cottage of golden stone with grey thatched roof lies in a fold of the snow-covered hills. Colour is given to the winter landscape by the dark emerald of the evergreens and the brilliant scarlet of holly berries. In the foreground, a tree stripped to winter bareness stands silhouetted against the pale sky.

WINTER COTTAGE

YOU WILL NEED

For the Winter Cottage picture, set in a mount with a cut-out measuring 16.5cm × 21.5cm (6½in × 8½in):

30cm × 35cm (12in × 14in) of antique white, 14-count Aida fabric
Stranded embroidery cotton in the colours given in the panel
No 26 tapestry needle
Wooden frame, measuring 26cm × 30cm (10⅜ × 12in)
Rectangular mount, cut to fit the frame, with cut-out as specified above
Strong thread and cardboard, for mounting

•

THE EMBROIDERY

Prepare the fabric as described on page 8; find the centre by folding, and mark the horizontal and vertical centre lines with basting stitches in a light-coloured thread. Set the fabric in a frame or hoop and count out from the centre to start stitching at a point convenient to you.

Two threads of cotton were used in the needle for cross stitches and one for backstitch *unless* otherwise stated in the colour key. Work all cross stitches first, and then the half crosses, taking them over one block of fabric. Make sure that all top stitches run in the same direction. Finally, work all backstitch details.

FINISHING

Gently handwash the finished piece, if necessary, and lightly press with a steam iron on the wrong side. Finally, stretch and mount the embroidery as explained on page 10. Insert it into the frame, behind the rectangular mount. A subtle wooden frame has been used for all four seasonal cottage pictures, and the colour of the mount has been especially selected in each case to echo colours predominant in the design.

WINTER COTTAGE ▶			DMC	ANCHOR	MADEIRA
Cross	Half Cross				
☒		Golden brown	612	832	2108
⬤		Medium golden brown	611	898	2107
☐		Medium beige grey	642	392	1906
◩		Light beige grey	644	830	1907
▲		Dark olive green	520	269	1514
N		Clear green	3363	262	1311
L		Medium grey green	522	859	1513
⊞	⊡	White	White	2	White
	⧄	Very pale grey	762	397	1804
	V	Silver grey	415	398	1803
Y		Scarlet	815	43	0513
⊘		Light scarlet	304	47	0509
◼		Very dark grey	844	401	1810
◪		Medium brownish grey	3022	8581	1903
I		Light brownish grey	3023	392	1902
◢		Tan	420	375	2104
T		Medium brown gold	372	855	211
⋀		Medium straw	3046	887	2206
	Z	Light blue grey	927	849	1708
		Dark brown*	839	360	1914

Note: bks house walls, door, roof, tree trunk, branches and birds with one strand of dark brown* (used for bks only), and window panes with two strands of white; when making half stitches with light blue grey, use one strand only.

$\mathscr{I}$NDEX

■

ACKNOWLEDGEMENTS

The authors would like to thank the following people for their help
and support during the preparation of the projects in this book:

Edith Cockrell, Joshua Cockrell, Lillie Cockrell, Tom Cockrell,
Julie Gill, Mike Grey, Lynda Hodgkinson, Elizabeth Marsh,
Ann Midwood, Sylvia Read, Cynthia Sherwood.

Thanks are also due to Coats Patons Crafts for supplying some of
the materials and threads used in the projects, to DMC for supplying
the Aida band on page 108, to Willow Fabrics, Knutsford for the
table linen on page 72, to Framecraft for supplying the basic items
needed for making up some of the projects and to 'Outlines' Picture
Framers of Clapham Common, London for framing the pictures on
pages 16, 46, 48, 56, 64, 124, 128, 132, 136.

SUPPLIERS

The following mail order
company has supplied some
of the basic items needed
for making up the projects in
this book:

Framecraft Miniatures Limited
372-376 Summer Lane
Hockley
Birmingham B19 3QA
England
Telephone 021 359 4442

*Addresses for Framecraft
stockists worldwide*
Ireland Needlecraft Pty Ltd
2-4 Keppel Drive
Hallam, Victoria 3803
Australia

Danish Art Needlework
PO Box 442, Lethbridge
Alberta T1J 3Z1
Canada

Sanyei Imports
PO Box 5, Hashima Shi
Gifu 501-62
Japan

The Embroidery Shop
286 Queen Street
Masterton
New Zealand

Anne Brinkley Designs Inc.
246 Walnut Street
Newton
Mass. 02160
USA

S A Threads and Cottons Ltd.
43 Somerset Road
Cape Town
South Africa

For information on your
nearest stockist of
embroidery cotton,
contact the following:

DMC

UK
DMC Creative World Limited
62 Pullman Road
Wigston, Leicester LE8 2DY
Telephone: 0533 811040

USA
The DMC Corporation
Port Kearney Bld.
10 South Kearney
NJ 07032-0650
Telephone: 201 589 0606

AUSTRALIA
DMC Needlecraft Pty
PO Box 317
Earlswood 2206
NSW 2204
Telephone: 02599 3088

COATS AND ANCHOR

UK
Kilncraigs Mill
Alloa
Clackmannanshire
Scotland FK10 1EG
Telephone: 0259 723431

USA
Coats & Clark
PO Box 27067
Dept CO1
Greenville
SC 29616
Telephone: 803 234 0103

AUSTRALIA
Coats Patons Crafts
Thistle Street
Launceston
Tasmania 7250
Telephone: 00344 4222

MADEIRA

UK
Madeira Threads (UK) Limited
Thirsk Industrial Park
York Road, Thirsk
N. Yorkshire YO7 3BX
Telephone: 0845 524880

USA
Madeira Marketing Limited
600 East 9th Street
Michigan City
IN 46360
Telephone: 219 873 1000

AUSTRALIA
Penguin Threads Pty Limited
25-27 Izett Street
Prahran
Victoria 3181
Telephone: 03529 4400